Praise for
Smart Is Not Enough!

Alan Guarino has always been a thought leader among retained search professionals, but now he proves he's also an expert in talent management. A must-read!

—Michael Foster, founder of the Human Capital Institute and author of *Recruiting on the Web*

If business is war, then Alan Guarino has cracked the code on how to make sure you have the talent needed to win. Don't miss this real-life guide written by one of the nation's leaders in the talent business.

—Kenneth Allard, author of *Business as War*

Business leadership requires a special mix of talent; Alan Guarino's book shows you how to optimize it.

—Paul Orfalea, founder of Kinko's and author of *Copy This!*

As an exceptional executive recruiter and leader, Alan Guarino has always been a valued contributor to business strategy. This book demonstrates his thought leadership in both business leadership and talent management.

—Jeanne L. Murtaugh, Vice Chairman, BNY Securities Group

SMART
☆☆ IS NOT ☆☆
ENOUGH!

SMART
☆☆ IS NOT ☆☆
ENOUGH!

The South Pole Theory and Other Powerful Talent Management Secrets

ALAN C. GUARINO

BICENTENNIAL
1807
WILEY
2007
BICENTENNIAL

John Wiley & Sons, Inc.

3 1257 01746 6169

Published by John Wiley & Sons, Inc., Hoboken, New Jersey.
Published simultaneously in Canada.

Wiley Bicentennial Logo: Richard J. Pacifico

For general information on our other products and services or for technical support,
please contact our Customer Care Department within the United States at
(800) 762-2974, outside the United States at (317) 572-3993 or fax (317) 572-4002.

Wiley also publishes its books in a variety of electronic formats. Some content that
appears in print may not be available in electronic books. For more information about
Wiley products, visit our web site at www.wiley.com.

ISBN 978-0-470-10010-3

Printed in the United States of America.

10 9 8 7 6 5 4 3 2 1

Contents

ACKNOWLEDGMENTS   ix

INTRODUCTION
Why You Need to Read This Book   xiii

PART I

THE TALENT CRISIS COULD BANKRUPT YOUR BUSINESS

1 THE GLOBAL TALENT MARKET
*Why Our Nation's Graduates Will Work for Wipro
in India and Why It Matters to Everyone*   3

2 THE PAST IS GONE, THE FUTURE IS NOW,
AND THE TALENT AGE IS UPON US   13

PART II

A SECRET SOURCE OF SUPERSTAR TALENT
ACADEMIC UNDERACHIEVERS
AND WHY SOME OF THEM
ARE WINNERS

3 HIRE FROM THE SOUTH POLE   27

4 EMOTIONAL INTELLIGENCE IS MORE IMPORTANT
THAN GRADE POINT AVERAGE   49

5 FIVE SOUTH POLE TALENT SECRETS   61

PART III
HUMAN CAPITAL
TALENT MANAGEMENT
HOW TO STRATEGIZE, ATTRACT, EVALUATE, DEVELOP, AND LEAD

6 THE HUMAN RESOURCES DIVISION
Finally, a Chance to Shine   81

7 STRATEGIZE TO OPTIMIZE TALENT
Talent Road Mapping and the Talent Inventory   99

8 ATTRACT SOUTH POLERS AND OTHER TALENT
Find the Needle in the Haystack   113

9 EVALUATE AND DEPLOY
Matching the Talent to the Mission and the Team   147

10 DEPLOY CUTTING-EDGE METHODS FOR
STAFF DEVELOPMENT
Invest in Human Capital   161

11 LEAD
Follow Me and Do as I Do   179

EPILOGUE   205

NOTES   207

INDEX   213

Acknowledgments

I told my friend John Grimaldi that I had a book in me, but someone had to pull it out. He did!

Richard Narramore, my editor at Wiley, made sure I actually had a book rather than just the rambling diary of a professional recruiter. He did what an editor is supposed to do and I am a better writer because of it. I am sure you all owe him your thanks as well—you would not have wanted to read my first attempt at this manuscript. Now, he and I hope that you won't be able to put this book down.

The book took shape around the topic of talent management in no small part because of my son Christofer. He showed me how a touch of dyslexia can make academic pursuits a major uphill battle for brilliant people. With an in-your-face attitude, he took on his last four years of high school and compressed them into three years. How he graduated high school in just three years, won an academic award, and attained "adequate" academic scores was amazing to watch. His triumph showed me the talents of the South Poler like I had never had the chance to observe before. The ultimate was the way he successfully *negotiated* acceptance into a highly ranked college when his academic scores precluded him from meeting the classic numbers-based admissions requirements. He sold himself in spite of his only slightly above average academic record. But that's what South Polers do. Chris is my hero!

While Chris gave me a living laboratory for the South Pole phenomenon, my daughter Allegra was my example of how to "Go for it!" She has never questioned which direction to head—she has made some course corrections, but the actual direction has never been in doubt. She showed me that living is not about *what* you do—your career—but about *who* you are—the person. Without this rudder, I would have taken a lot more time before "looking up" from my career and there is much I would have missed by then. Allegra is my champion!

A family friend recently told me he was always impressed by the things I did in my business life. He then looked at my wife and said, "as much as Alan has impressed me, I'm more impressed with you." He was right. She is much smarter than me—and she is certainly better looking and very strong. Kathy gave our business its legs. In business, she kept me from the deep end when it looked inviting. She made sure the *risk* always had a *reward*. She did the hard, tedious stuff that people like me take for granted while she simultaneously somehow raised two amazing kids in a very difficult world. Kathy is my oxygen!

A recent *Time* magazine cover story explored how your siblings make you who you are. Although I have never told them, I never doubted that my sisters, Amy and Marie, made me who I am. They filled me with confidence and attention, slapped me around when I got a little full of myself, and showed me where the limits were. They are the best kind of winners—the ones who speak with their actions.

My mom is the one who showed me the way, while my dad showed me how to work—like it or not. They are two of the most amazing people God has ever created. They are the best role models in the world—devoted, humble, smart, caring, and honest. I will never match their success.

There are a few others who require mentioning—Donna Cornell, one of the best recruiters ever, my former boss and the person who taught me to recruit; Dan Gonzalez, a great recruiter and Cornell's longest tenured staff member; Bev Jacobson, my first real client; Andrea Cattani (now Diamond), who introduced me to New York's top executive search professionals; she should come back to this business "someday"; Tom Perna, who hired me onto Wall Street; and Ray Roe, who bought our company.

Rather than acknowledging other colleagues from my work life, other family members, my in-laws, and friends, I simply acknowledge that they know who they are and that I'd give them the shirt off my back if they needed it. I would certainly miss someone's name if I tried to make a list, so I'm chickening out!

Introduction: Why You Need to Read This Book

When it comes to the folks in the business world, I'm sorry to say that I don't hold too many in high regard. Maybe it's an occupational hazard—I evaluate people for a living. It's my job. The individuals who constitute this world of employees, managers, and executives were all hired by someone and that hiring process has in part supported a basic level of mediocrity. The good news is that I have seen employers change the way they think about and handle the hiring process. They have gotten much more serious about making selections, laboring over each hiring decision. They constantly seek more data and more insight so that the person they hire has been analyzed under a microscope.

HUMAN PROSPECTING AND THE SOUTH POLE PHENOMENON

We are now in the Talent Age. This book demonstrates that the Information Age is over. It shows you the latest approaches to optimizing talent—how your competitors are doing it in ways you may never have imagined. How about coaching techniques where employees are hooked up to machines that measure biological readings during certain situations? How about software that takes the emotional pulse of hundreds of employees in just three minutes every week and synthesizes that data into a one-page report to the organization's management? One executive who uses this evaluation tool says that he saved his organization $17 million as a result.

Today, businesses and organizations need amazing people just to hold their ground. And every element of the talent management process, from strategy to hiring to developing, deploying, evaluating, and leading must be operating at peak effectiveness. I will show you ways to do this. But beyond tools and techniques, there is also a secret weapon—a special pool of talent that can be better optimized.

Where is this talent pool? I'll explain it this way. Smart is simply not enough these days. Smart is only part of it. We need to continue our time-honored approach of hiring academic achievers. However, we need an even bigger arsenal of talent to compete in the future. Surprisingly, a significant percentage of academic *underachievers* have also made great CEOs, leaders, managers, and entrepreneurs—this has always been the case. So when it comes to picking talent, why is it that we seem only to pay attention to GPAs, SATs, and other grades that show how well a person can score on a test? Because it's hard to measure talent in other ways, we look for the best and the brightest at the top of the class: That's not a bad idea, but it's not enough.

I completely disagree with the concept that the "best and the brightest" will have high GPAs. It's not that easy. The fact is that the best and the brightest sometimes have high GPAs and sometimes have low GPAs or no GPAs. In the twenty-first century, where the survival of an organization or business hinges on the quality of its talent, you need to open your mind and think about talent as a critical resource and leave no stone unturned. There are many valedictorians working for people who they outscored on SATs and other tests. By understanding this, you can find ways to beat your competitors in the talent game.

I call these academic underachievers *South Polers*. They are the ones who, during their careers, somehow outperform their more studious colleagues. They are South Polers because they are the small group of talent buried in the large group at the bottom half of every academic class. If the world of talent is round, they reside at the *southern pole* of their class when it is ranked academically. They are the special pool of talent we need to identify and capitalize on. I offer much more on this topic later in the book.

There was a fellow born in Revere, Massachusetts, in 1832. In his 20s, the Civil War raged, but he was rejected by the Union Army because of his asthma. His interests shifted him toward teaching as well as becoming a newspaper correspondent in Europe for the Boston *Transcript* and the New York *Sun*. In 1864, he returned to North America to become a Unitarian minister and, later, a social service worker in New York. This was the New York of the Great Immigration. Ellis Island was in full swing. Economic and political refugees were flooding into the Lower East Side, some trickling out to the rest of the nation. The slums of lower Manhattan were beyond belief. If you were lucky, you got your family into a firetrap without windows. The streets teemed with children speaking every imaginable language. The prim and proper people in America were in shock. This was a disgrace. Most of these people were poorly educated and some could not even speak the language of their new home. Let's just say that if you ran, say, a bank at this time, you were not likely to look to this particular pool of talent for your next CFO or even your janitor.

But this young minister from Revere saw something different. He saw the devastating poverty, and people with the deck stacked against them. It was hard to miss. But he also saw opportunity, life, creativity, and many hard-working, eager, savvy people who were happy to have landed in America, filled with ambition and the vigor to strive.

The gentleman from Revere was named Horatio Alger and he went on to earn a fortune writing dime novels about people from these very slums transforming themselves from rags to riches, thanks to the business and social opportunities in America. Alger coined the very notion of people pulling themselves up by their bootstraps. And do you know what? His fiction turned into reality, as thousands of immigrants went on to make very good—and some fabulous— lives for themselves and their descendants. These folks began their business lives in the South Pole of society, yet they achieved and outperformed others who were more privileged. Why? They were able to do so because of their special talents—their savvy, not just their smarts.

Horatio Alger saw not dirt but gold in those slums. Alger firmly believed that through honesty, hard work, and strong determination, the American Dream was available to anyone willing and able to make the journey. Sure they had to be smart, but they were not academically anointed. That is still what makes America great, and it is what makes American businesses great, too; that is, if you (like Alger) know how to dig gold out of the teeming masses of prospective employees.

Most everyone in every job today is part of a team, either formally or informally. The team represents the collective of each individual talent on the team. Any manager, team member, or executive who understands the nuances of talent, its behaviors, and its substance will have a major advantage over those with whom they compete.

I don't mince words—I have been known to say that far too many people who go to work every day are *liabilities*

rather than *assets* to their organizations. I believe that up-
wards of perhaps 20 percent to 40 percent of so-called executives and managers are empty suits who avoid responsibility,
jump on band wagons once the winning idea is clear, and
generally find ways to live mediocre business lives and get
paid for it. Over the past 15 years, as an executive search
professional and business leader, I have made a career out
of evaluating talent—"inspecting the goods" of people at almost every level in the management hierarchy of businesses
and organizations. I have made my share of mistakes as well.
Talent is the blood of any organization—without it, the organization is no more than a business plan waiting to be ex-
ecuted. People have finally reemerged as the most valuable
resource in the business world today. For a short time, machines and computers won out over people. In this book, I
show you why it is the talent—the people—who you need to
invest in.

I've been fortunate to spend most of my adult life in
leadership roles. At the age of 26, I commanded a U.S. Army,
armored cavalry troop in the 1980s during the Cold War. At
the age of 33, with little direct experience in the field, I
started a human resource consulting and retained executive
search firm with virtually zero capital. I ran the company as
my team and I scaled the firm to industry prominence on
Wall Street, profitably managed it through my industry's
most tumultuous era, and then successfully sold the company to the largest recruiting company in the world. I have
been involved as an advisor to many start-up businesses as
well as two large businesses that grew by hundreds of millions of dollars. I recruited for them and assisted them with
business strategy and acquisitions. The small companies I
have been involved with have gone public or have been sold
to companies like Aon and Omnicom. I have learned one
thing: Great business plans mean very little; great people

can make weak businesses fly; and mediocre talent can drive a great business to its knees. This is true now more than ever before.

The Information Age is over; the Talent Age is here. If you are on a team or if you lead a team, you need to know what I will share with you in the coming chapters. Today, Alger's teeming masses aren't gone; they have simply been transformed into college students, drop-outs, and graduates who vie for positions in your organization. Can you find the gold? Once the gold is found, it needs to be deployed, evaluated, developed, and led. No leader ever succeeds alone. As a matter of fact, I see it from the complete opposite perspective. I see that when a team succeeds, the by-product is that the leader succeeds. I subscribe to the adage: *team fails; leader fails; game over.*

I told my publisher that I wanted this book to be just like the great college professor who we were all lucky to have on occasion—the one who made learning fun, whose class we really wanted to attend, who did not preach at us but provoked us, and who got us fired up to think rather than just to study. I hope that is what we have achieved in this book. If reading it gets slow, just hang on because I promise the next paragraph will grab your attention and make you want to read on.

☆☆ The Talent Crisis ☆☆
Could Bankrupt
Your Business

1

☆ ☆ The Global ☆ ☆
Talent Market

Why Our Nation's Graduates Will Work for Wipro in India and Why It Matters to Everyone

The need of a constantly expanding market for its products chases the bourgeoisie over the whole surface of the globe. It must nestle everywhere, settle everywhere, and establish connections everywhere. The bourgeoisie has through its exploitation of the world market given a cosmopolitan character to production and consumption in every country. . . . It compels all nations, on pain of extinction, to adopt the bourgeois mode of production; it compels them to introduce what it calls civilization into their midst, that is, to become bourgeois themselves. In one word, it creates a world after its own image.

— Marx and Engels, *The Communist Manifesto*

S top! Go back and read the Introduction or you won't understand what I mean when I use the term *South Poler*. Personally, I rarely read the Introduction of a book. I've never been that patient. I always want to get right to the good stuff. In this book, the Introduction has some of the good stuff. If you have already read it—congratulations, you're a better person than I am. If you have not, go back and read it.

Exactly what day was it when the world changed? When did we go from Mayberry to a Brave New World? I know it happened in my lifetime, but I'm not sure exactly when. I remember when there were barbershops that thrived and family-run clothing stores that were just fine when we needed a suit. I remember that the phrase *online* was used when you were waiting to check out at the grocery store. I know that there was a time when people worked for the same corporation for their entire careers. There was even a time when a corporate executive still had time to join a bowling league, volunteer at the firehouse, or have three martinis at lunch. They had the time and could afford to be unproductive for half the day. Today, people productivity has changed radically. The most precious commodity businesses seek now is talent, and it is being optimized in ways never seen before.

However, there is still an underutilized, secret pool of talent that has never been actively sought or cultivated—*South Polers*—the select few, exceptional individuals found among the masses of students ranked in the bottom half of their academic classes. That's right; in the bottom half of every class are some of the most brilliant, driven, innovative people on the planet. They can take your business to the next level, but the catch is they're hard to find. In the coming chapters, I tell you more about the need to invest in both the talent and the opportunity that these South Polers offer us as we seek to remain competitive.

GLOBALIZATION IS ABOUT MORE THAN OUTSOURCING AND THE INTERNET

Not since the Industrial Revolution have we faced greater change in the operating environment of business. Our talent issues truly span the world. The boundless labor market has made the *Fortune* 500 more profitable and more nimble. Today, even a small business can contemplate outsourcing its routine activities to third parties. A real estate agency with only a few agents can now have its phone lines answered by a virtual assistant in India at a fraction of the cost of a local service. The opportunities for the use of talent are endless and talent is no longer constricted by traditional boundaries. None of this should be a surprise; in many ways, Marx predicted this sort of market forces-driven expansion a century ago—he saw that the world would "flatten" and he was not happy about it.

The term *globalization* has been beaten to death in countless business books, but very few authors have talked about how globalization impacts talent—how talent must be mined, cultivated, reinvented, fine-tuned, and otherwise optimized. All the previous discussions of talent and globalization have focused on outsourcing jobs to lower-cost labor markets. Actually, talent is now a key form of business capital, perhaps more important than financial capital. Will talent be the ultimate advantage? Will talent be the resource that makes the difference when all the demographics and statistical analyses predict otherwise? Will it once again and finally be all about the people?

KARL, WE HARDLY KNEW YE

You've really got to hand it to Karl Marx—few writers in history have messed up quite as badly. He was an intelligent guy and wrote a brilliant analysis of the capitalist system of his time, but his projections for the future were almost completely wrong. Karl Marx is a classic example of the genius who just didn't have the savvy. Being smart was not enough. He was too caught up in his own negative emotional response to the capitalism he saw around him to be able to see the good in it. He also was naive about human beings. James Madison said that if men were angels, the world would not need government. To work, socialism requires a race of entirely selfless people. When the early Communist leaders realized that their citizens were all too human, they didn't scrap their ideology. They thought that they could indoctrinate children to *become* perfect citizens who really would be happy under the Communist system.

Although you may have seen the last of Karl Marx, the contest for global economic supremacy is alive and well. A century ago, Marx and the other neophyte Communists thought the battle would be between the workers and the industrialists. This probably made some sense at the time. The Industrial Revolution was finally in full swing and fat cats during the Gilded Age were raking in fortunes by hiring workers for pennies and working those workers long hours. At one point in Chicago, under intense market pressure, the Pullman railroad car company was paying some of its full-time workers 12 cents a week. In a sense,

Marx was right. This model couldn't last, and the enlightened capitalist countries instituted a few reforms (a few too many for some employers, but that's another discussion).

Marx envisioned a worldwide battle with the workers ultimately defeating the capitalists, leading to a universal worker's utopia. Something more or less the opposite is now happening. The capitalists are themselves engaged in a worldwide battle for economic supremacy—not because corporations are out to get the other guy, but simply as a result of Darwinian forces. The world's corporations are going through a process similar to what finches and turtles went through (and, I suppose, are still going through) on the Galapagos Islands. There are only so many resources in the world and the fitter contestant is going to grab them and survive.

Evolutionwise, the United States and U.S. business have enjoyed about a half-century head start in the new global economy. Europe and Asia essentially committed economic suicide during World War II, leaving North America, and in particular the United States, as the only global player without crushing war debt or a demolished infrastructure. The Russians and the Chinese, on top of this, adopted a hopelessly naive economic model. Europe has now recovered physically from the war, and Russia and China are throwing off their outdated economic theories. Now is when the real battle begins. Now is when we will see if Europe and America really do have the right stuff, as they engage on a more level playing field.

It's a Flat World after All

Up until *New York Times* columnist Thomas Friedman wrote his recent book, *The World Is Flat,* on how the competitive business world is flattening out, flat worlders were generally known as people who genuinely believed that the earth is not a sphere and that the Apollo trips to the moon were staged on a Hollywood back lot.[1] Unfortunately, those of us still living in the real world are unable to retreat into reassuring fantasy. And the world really is "flat" now, as Friedman describes, at least economically. What Friedman essentially means is that there's no place left to hide in the world, least of all North America. Everybody's playing in the same pool now. The United States can no longer indulge in economic xenophobia, producing and consuming primarily for itself. Whatever the big guys do now directly affects all of the little guys. The ripples are felt throughout the entire global pond. There may be some aboriginal tribes left lurking in the Amazon jungle someplace, but the last ones I heard about just got cell phones.

The United States and its European Union (EU) business partners are no longer writing the economic rules, at least not completely. For the time being, we are still the 800-pound global economic gorilla, but the possibility now looms that if we don't play our cards right, we could be left out of the new loop. In the new global economy, the United States, if it doesn't find the right way to compete with the right human capital, could become an economic backwater. That is impossible you say? I bet the Romans felt the same way—until those elephants came rumbling over the Alps.

AMERICA'S PLIGHT IS REFLECTIVE OF MOST OTHER MATURE ECONOMIES

So what are America's chances in the new global economy? American business has become very efficient. Corporate America is doing more with less; but that, in and of itself, won't be enough. What do I mean? The executive today and the management layers below the executive team are being asked to do much more with much less management infrastructure than in years gone by. Corporate America has flattened. Gone are the layers and layers of hierarchy found in the IBMs and the GEs of the 1950s, 1960s, 1970s, and 1980s. The *company man* of once-popular business school teachings in organizational psychology is gone. That double-speaking bureaucrat has been replaced by air—not hot air, but *dead* air—on the organization chart. His job is gone and there is nothing in its place. In the 1960s, 1970s, 1980s, and even the 1990s, corporate America was a world cloistered from global competition. We saw the world as a source of resources (gold, copper, cheap labor, oil), and also a place to sell our finished goods and services. We had huge economic world dominance—or at least parity with other major economic powers. We *talked* about global competition in graduate school; it was really just theory. But in the past six years or so, global competition has truly surfaced. No more *theory.*

Why is this important? Well, for one very practical reason—American business is about to face a level of competition that exceeds the imagination. It will shake us to the very core of our business ethos and for the first time we will truly face a talent shortage at the management level.

If you think that Japan's meteoric rise in the auto industry over just three decades is scary, you haven't seen anything yet. Japan, roughly ⅟₁₀₀ the size of the United States in geographic area, with a fraction of the resources of India and China, handed the U.S. auto industry a major blow. Just imagine what two competitors—who combined are about 33 times *larger* than Japan—are going to be able to do. They will not only be chasing our customers but also our management talent. On the topic of leadership talent in his China operations, Tom Johnson, former CEO of Chesapeake Corp, was quoted in *Fortune* magazine as saying, "They are constantly getting stolen away . . . labor is abundant, but management is scarce."[2] So remember the basics of supply and demand and ask what will happen as these markets mature and look to our shores for a critical resource, TALENT.

While growing their own talent (India and China produce a combined 4.4 million college graduates each year to our 1.3 million), they will also be recruiting away our talent to join their multinational-global companies. This is something few college graduates in the 1950s, 1960s, 1970s, and 1980s even contemplated. Do you know any who said that when they graduated in 1970 they really wanted to join Wipro, the information technology (IT) company from India? No, they wanted to join AT&T—you know, the giant of the telephone industry—which has long since been hammered from every competitive direction. Others joined Chrysler—you remember that U.S. company—which is now part of a German conglomerate. The modern world has come full circle. In the early years of the market economy, tradespeople and artisans drove the market based on their skill to produce appealing products. Machinery then supplanted the individual, and a business's machinery and automation became more important than the person behind the machine. Again, technology (IT) made this machinery and people even more effective, and it was the IT investment that made or broke the business. All that may have finally run its course directly back to the one thing people cannot mass produce—talent. Because of the efficiency of our capital markets, most businesses can buy all the machinery and IT they need. So what will make the difference? Talent will make the difference, but there is one thing we need to realize: Talent is in drastically short supply. We have created very complex jobs that call for exceptional people.

Isn't it a good idea to leave no stone unturned when developing or recruiting management talent? Isn't it a good idea to reform some bad habits and make sure we optimize our threatened pool of human capital? This holds true for our friends in Europe as well. Maybe even more so if you subscribe to Pete Cappelli's views from his book *The New Deal at Work*. Yes, that's right—the United States and Europe will be challenged beyond belief. Managers and senior executives will need to understand this sea change, or sink.

But, understand it or not, our graduates will have options a lot farther away than our coasts—they'll be sought by the Wipros in India and others not yet known in China and Eastern Europe. This is important to ALL of us.

2

☆☆ The Past Is Gone, ☆☆
the Future Is Now, and
the Talent Age Is
upon Us

In the twenty-first century, talent will be a greater differentiator than technology or financial capital! But don't take my word for it. Just look at the facts illustrated in the stock market; it is numbers, not opinions that prove the point. Just look at the numbers.

For at least two centuries, financial capital was the most important asset in building shareholder wealth. Now, human capital may just be the most important asset. Microsoft has created at least $140 billion in shareholder wealth deploying less than $35 billion in capital. Larger, more industrial companies whose productivity is driven by capital equipment have deployed significantly more financial capital to achieve less in shareholder wealth. If you doubt this, take a look at Ford or ExxonMobil. So what do the numbers tell us? Very simply that if a company has a significant market capitalization and deploys relatively small amounts of financial capital to achieve it, the wealth must be coming from some other form of capital. The revelation today is that the real wealth builders achieve success from human capital, not financial capital. So what does that mean for the future?

In the twentieth century, companies actually survived with mediocre, barely adequate management talent (smart but not too savvy), allowing companies with *exceptional* management talent to actually hit the cover off the ball. In the twenty-first century, however, exceptional management is *required* for survival, and only star-studded management will overachieve. I've already mentioned that for the first time in history, American executive and management talent will have abundant options beyond our shores. We now compete in a truly global marketplace for the first time in world history. We talked about being global in the 1980s, and 1990s but in the 2000s we are truly global. The rules have changed, the stakes have gotten higher, and *all* the people who manage the company must overachieve at all levels. In the twenty-first century, *smart is simply not enough.* I can sum it up this way: Previously, if your manufacturing equipment was inferior, your competitor could build a better product more efficiently. Now if your human capital is inferior, your competitor will beat your company in creating products and services. It is that simple. Financial capital has become less important, and human capital has become the discriminator.

Competition has become so intense that we just don't have enough *exceptional* talent ready to deploy. I'll give you an example: Think about the professional athlete in the 1940s and 1950s. Compare him or her to the professional athlete of today. How many professional athletes from the 1940s and 1950s could have been stars today? Probably not many. Athletes compete against technologically tuned competitors who are much more savvy and sophisticated in their training regimens and their competitive techniques than in years gone by. Western business faces the same sophistication from its competitors, but with a shrinking talent pool. That's what corporations are facing today—more sophisticated competition with less talent to pull from. I'm talking about talent, not just demographics. I don't know if our labor pool will have enough *bodies*—I really don't care about that as much as whether we'll actually have enough *talent.*

Deloitte Consulting has been on top of this and in one of their white papers had this eye-opening statistic to pass along:

> The U.S. Department of Education estimates that 60 percent of all new jobs in the twenty-first century will require skills that

are possessed by only 20 percent of the current workforce. Local shortages of critical talent mean companies will have to source talent across a global market.

And just what is the solution they propose for this new dilemma? Deloitte says, "Shift your mindset. The talent game has changed and traditional talent management processes haven't kept up. They are too inflexible, too costly (companies spend 50 times more on recruiting than training)."

WESTERN TALENT IS UNDER ATTACK

For business people, global issues in just the past few years have become more relevant than they have ever been. We've been *talking* about it for a decade at least, and it's finally here in a big way.

How about this example? Over a recent 48-hour period, I took an informal sample of our customers' recruiting inquiries. During that time, the last three clients that contacted us in New York wanted to recruit people in Asia—these were American companies looking for executive talent in Asia and having difficulty. That's not all that earth-shattering—Western companies are building a bigger foothold in Asia every day. During that same 48-hour period, one of our colleagues in our Indian business unit called us about an Indian company that needed us to find executive talent for their expanding automotive industry business on three continents simultaneously; in Germany, Japan, and the United States. In 1944, the United States and its allies launched the D-Day offensive on only one continent. This is corporate D-Day times three and all from an Indian company expanding in the automotive industry. Go ahead; name three top Indian automobile product brands. You can't today, but you will soon. The global marketplace is a true reality and not from the way we envisioned it in graduate school. It is not just a place to buy our goods and services and for us to find cheap labor. The global marketplace is a real, viable, and serious threat to our human capital—our talent pool. As the lesser developed countries build viable economies, they will establish new business operations with real white-collar jobs and real career paths. All this will just increase the need for talent. We are now in a global marketplace—not just for goods and services, but for talent.

Some believe that U.S. business rivals in the coming global economic battle will be the European Union (EU) and Asia. The former Soviet Union, though frightening militarily, will be no threat economically. I do believe that this reality is still a ways off. First, let's assess the threat from the EU. I recall reading in a recent magazine article that the new Europe, with its common currency and open borders, looks like the United States more than it resembles anything in European history. So, the EU shows some promise in becoming a threat to American business. The EU's economic clout is becoming increasingly stronger through the European-owned corporations that produce many "American" consumer products, such as A&W Root Beer.

How did America go from being threatened by Russian ICBMs to being threatened by European root beer? There are stranger things yet to come in the new world economy. If there's one traditional American trait that will have to come to the fore it's bronco busting. We've just got to mount up and try to tame the wild thing underneath us. But we will need to have a few atypical bronco busters on the team. A management team made up of the bronco busters of old will not stay on until the whistle blows. Put some South Polers on that team and watch the team beat the whistle.

The EU looks like a major threat, but the article goes on to point out that they have an Achilles heel such as double-digit unemployment, a declining birthrate, and a union-dominated quasi-socialist welfare state. The EU has the know-how and the economic infrastructure to compete, but may lack the people or the ideology. Like the United States, the EU's fate will rest on talent issues more than anything else.

The other threats, China and India, are in a sense the mirror image of the EU. In Asia, they have very little existing business infrastructure, but they do have many ambitious, hard-working people. For decades, America's large consumer population essentially drove the world market. Most of China and India today are impoverished, but with their stratospheric economic growth rates, it won't be that long before companies will design their products with the Chinese consumer in mind, not the American. And in India, they already speak the new international language—English.

So globalization is real, and the threats of Europe and Asia are coming, but they're not here quite yet. We know that a fierce economic global competition is on the horizon, but people don't universally agree on the looming talent shortage. When people talk about the growing competitiveness of global business, they talk about copper and energy shortages: Build more oil refinery capacity; dig more mines. When was the last time that talent prices and availability was discussed on the evening news? Where is the "Talent Futures Index"?

Peter Capelli in his book *The New Deal at Work* makes a clear and compelling case against the talent shortage in the United States by using demographic data—pure, solid head counting.[1] The Human Capital Institute, in its human capital strategist training program, makes the opposite case using demographics—pure head counting. Who is right? Neither or both—in and of itself, it doesn't matter because we should be measuring the amount of *talent*, not just the number of heads. It's about the numbers, but it's also about the *quality* of the talent. We need to know if we have enough people entering the labor pool; however, these people also need to be talented and led and managed by super-talented, savvy leaders. We need future employees, managers, and executive talent, but unlike past generations the North Pole will not produce enough. It doesn't produce enough now. Let Peter Capelli, the Human Capital Institute, and others report on the numbers and do the highly quantitative analysis that is valuable on an enterprisewide basis. It is indeed an important part of the work that needs to be done. But as a headhunter, I'll tell you to get creative about the talent, or the numbers won't matter. Huge markets and fiercely competitive global corporations will engage in the ultimate Darwinian competition.

Will the West Seed the World with Talent?

Just imagine this likely, soon-to-be scenario: Little Johnny and Mary have just graduated from an elite U.S. university and they are overjoyed to have landed plum jobs—in Singapore and Beijing. Both Johnny and Mary have been diligently learning several new languages and are off to make their fortunes overseas, though they'll probably still come home for the holidays.

In the new global economy, the top talent will hold all the cards and be able to call the shots. We have been so worried in the United States about foreign talent invading our shores and jobs being sent overseas that we lost sight of the very real likelihood that the best native-born American corporate talent is likely to join in the new global competitive market and move to wherever the best opportunity is. The top U.S. graduates are no longer going to decide whether to live on the East or West Coasts, but on which continent. And why shouldn't they? It's just as easy to call from and fly home from Paris as it is from Manhattan. Americans in general resist entering the global economy and learning new languages, but that won't apply to our more nimble offspring. They're going to recognize opportunity and work hard to make it—whatever it takes—as they always have.

But it is far easier for Johnny and Mary to pull up stakes and move to Singapore, Hong Kong, New Delhi, or wherever, than it is for Sony to move to Beijing or for General Motors to move to Berlin. The new global corporations themselves are going to be far less mobile than their new employees. So companies will have to engage in a truly global competition for the best managers and executives. This will make talent recruitment not only far more crucial but also far more difficult. Companies will have to have their feelers out to the entire planet. This is much more complicated than placing a want ad in the *New York Times* and then sifting through the resumes that come in. Remember those days? That was not so long ago.

The principals of supply and demand will govern a worldwide talent market; entry level, executive, and management talent will not be exempt. In the *McKinsey Quarterly,* an article titled "How India's Executives See the World"[2] provides some valuable data and graphics. Business leaders across India share an upbeat vision of the future while recognizing the obstacles ahead (see Box).

We in the United States, particularly when it comes to business, have a tendency to forget about the rest of the world, except as a potential market for our products. For decades, we have been the producers and "they" have been the buyers. This is no longer true. We can no longer afford to be so xenophobic in our business calculations—especially, when it comes to talent.

One instructive example of this is the issue of outsourcing. So many people in the United States are horrified at outsourcing. We're losing all of our manufacturing. Indeed, we are. But what if, instead of losing a couple of tire manufacturing plants, we were losing most of the brightest (and savviest) graduates of our universities? Well, that's what most of the rest of the world has been suffering at our hands for decades.

By and large, executives in India think that the opening up of the global economy presents them with huge opportunities for growth. A *McKinsey Quarterly* survey, which polled more than 9,300 executives around the world, including 537 in India, shows that Indian business leaders are much more optimistic about the future than are their international peers.* Yet rather surprisingly for a country with one of the world's largest labor pools, they see the high cost and low availability of talent as the single greatest constraint on their companies—a problem that worries them much more than it does their counterparts around the world.

---

*Erica J. Bever, Elizabeth Stephenson, and David W. Tanner, "How India's Executives See the World," *McKinsey Quarterly* (Special Edition, 2005).

While we may worry about that brilliant Indian software engineer taking a job away from our little Johnny in Silicon Valley, what do you think they're thinking in New Delhi? They've just lost another of their best and brightest—gone to help the United States succeed in the new global economy and not India.

American business needs to stop thinking that it's only all about them. The rest of the globe does not exist simply to cater to U.S. business' every whim. We've got to start being a real team player on the global stage. We've got to *stop* being so self-centered and *start* being more savvy, or the United States will disproportionately seed the world with talent.

TALENT: THE OLD GOLD STANDARD COMES FULL CIRCLE

I contend that the twenty-first century has indeed begun the Talent Age—or, more appropriately, the return of the Talent Age. Here's a little history lesson.

In early years of the colonies in America, the most prized products were sold by craftspeople. This was true in Europe and in all early commercial markets. These artisans were the gold standard of quality and the producers of valuable items used in the home and the creation of larger goods: The cooper built the wheels for the wagon; the silversmith fashioned the finery for the tables of the wealthy and made the utensils for the tables of the more humble souls, too. Other than the things people made for themselves, the goods and services sold in the marketplace somehow came from the work of a talented individual.

Now, fast-forward a little more than a century or so. Machinery came to replace the talent of the craftsperson. Mass production machinery allowed less talented people to fashion those goods that craftspeople had once made. Talent became less important. This machinery allowed for progress—lower priced goods, greater employment opportunities for unskilled labor, and more goods available to the marketplace, thus reducing scarcities. The machinery offered an advantage over the craftsperson. It became the item that was critical for success and put craftspeople out of business. The machinery became the gold standard for the underpinning of the business. Individual talent was less critical.

Okay, fast-forward another 50 years. Technology now appears—the computer made the machinery even more efficient. It automated production lines so that less people were needed to run the machines. Indeed, technology even made those people with the green eyeshades more efficient at crunching numbers.

It made the people in the purchasing department more efficient. Technology made the sales and marketing teams more efficient. Some of the slower-to-adapt companies found that their competitors were able to win by adopting these technologies. For both service businesses and industrial businesses, companies were acquired or put out of business because of missteps in the adoption of technology. Technology revolutionized the production of goods and services yet again.

Name a company today that competes in the industrial sector without using machinery. Name a services company today that does not use technology. You can't—they all do. Some more effectively than others, but they all do. Yet these devices are no longer able to offer significant competitive advantage. Especially in the services sector, the competitive advantage is again the *talent*.

Those with the best talent will win. I hope I've aroused your competitive juices. Can you afford to overlook any potential source of talent? Can you continue to throw entry-level South Polers to the wolves, or should you *cultivate* the young ones and *recruit* the experienced ones who've already begun to make their mark?

What do you think?

☆☆ A Secret Source ☆☆ of Superstar Talent: Academic Underachievers and Why Some of Them Are Winners

3

☆ ☆ Hire from the ☆ ☆ South Pole

The world is moving so fast these days that the man who says it can't be done is generally interrupted by someone doing it.

—Elbert Hubbard

Talent has really taken on a whole new meaning, finally coming of age as an asset. Remember the blustering managers of old who said, "Our people are the company's most important asset" and then spent relative pennies on training and developing them? Those types will be crushed in the next wave of business evolution. But before you can train and develop the talent, you have to acquire it. Actually, you have to attract it, but more about that later. For now, let's take a look at the secret source of talent that most businesses have overlooked for the past 75 years or more. With talent in short supply, this could be the key to your organization's future success. It's like mining for gold—you have to sift through a great deal of material to find the rare piece of gold, but the cost of the sifting is more than offset by the reward.

I Call It Savvy—Call It What You Want, Just Hire It

Have you ever wondered why some people seem to rise above the crowd with seemingly little effort? Have you ever wondered why valedictorians find themselves working for people who graduated much lower in their classes?

Success, defined as business achievement, comes to a wide range of people. For some, it has little correlation to their classroom successes. In his book *Copy This,* the founder of Kinko's says:

> With so much emphasis on SAT scores and 4.0 Grade Point Averages I think our schools and universities are selecting out the resilient kids, eliminating all the students like me. We've created a system geared to advancing the test takers.[1]

If these people do not appear to be smart, how *do* they succeed? They *are* smart—most have at least a reasonable IQ level, but they also have a significant amount of something else. What is it? The founder of Kinko's gives us a clue:

> Straight-A types unaccustomed to failure enter the marketplace and take their first belly flops especially hard. They're so shocked they don't know how to react. Why do you think so many of them go back to graduate school? It's a huge relief to return to the safety of a system through which they can navigate.[2]

This phenomenon is of interest to more than me and the founder of Kinko's. In efforts to provide scientific explanations, some academics are pursuing this topic. There is the emotional intelligence (EI) theory put forward by Daniel Goleman in the mid-1990s that tries to explain what drives achievement beyond IQ. In addition to Goleman's views, another professor, Robert J. Sternberg, formerly at Yale, labels this phenomenon "practical intelligence." I will not dwell on the complexities of their academic work. They do a fine job explaining their theories. I simply want to awaken business leaders to a highly talented pool of people they have never seriously targeted—academic underachievers.

The noted author Thomas Friedman makes a case that "the world is flat." I agree when it comes to business-to-business competition. But when it comes to talent, the world is *round* with two very important poles—the North Pole, where the top-ranked academics achievers are found, and the South Pole, where bright and *savvy* winners are found. Although this was not the case in the past, you now need both poles on your team if you are to succeed as a twenty-first-century business leader.

Don't get me wrong, I have great respect for academic achievement—just ask my kids at report card time. However, when it comes to building the team that, under the CEO's guidance, will make or break the company, I encourage a balanced team, including people who succeed because they are South Polers. This is also true of the teams well below the company's C suite; everyone on a team needs to understand this source of talent. Understanding the South Pole phenomenon is critical to optimizing an organization's talent. South Polers are bright people who have not scored well academically, but who have the ability to achieve great things in business. Their achievement stems from other capabilities that are not scored in GPAs and SATs—a sort of magic.

Some people cheapen this magic by labeling it *street smarts*. That term kindles thoughts of a streetwise thug or some two-bit loan shark. I like to refer to this talent as business *savvy* or *magic*. Some North Polers possess both academic brilliance and business savvy. There have been plenty in the ranks of the world's great corporate leaders. They have been CEOs, CFOs, sales leaders, and top-ranked managers and scientists. But there is a precious, yet difficult-to-find pool of talent buried at the opposite pole. The South Pole is where a few smart people with exceptional business savvy reside. They don't stand out in GPA ranking, but they will achieve great things with or without corporate backing. It's best for you if these South Polers are on your team.

I can summarize it this way. Have you ever heard of *business savvy* conveyed in the context of the person's academic brilliance? I think not. Most often, it is conveyed as *charisma*—but it's much more than that. This savvy is an intangible because academic measures can't score it, but savvy can be found through careful evaluation and you do need to find it. Whatever you call it, it's a powerful component of the success equation: IQ + Business savvy = Winner. While IQ or high GPA alone equals a smart person who will ultimately work *for* someone *with* strong business savvy; smart is not enough.

How Do You Define a Winner in Business?

Many CEOs will tell you that winners are the people who simply get the job done, all the while motivating their staff and actually having some fun. *Simply* getting the job done. Boy, is that an understatement. Globalization in the twenty-first century has made *getting the job done* nothing less than miraculous. That is a key point. We have created jobs at virtually all levels in the knowledge-worker chain that require exceptional performance if the job is to be done right. It's almost as if organizations need an all-star player in every role or there is a breakdown. We have reached a point, much like it has always been in the military, where the organization truly is only as strong as its weakest link. In the past, that weak link could be tolerated as "good enough"; the organization could get by and compensate. No longer is this the case; the business world is way too competitive for that. The competition is too savvy. You need winners at all levels in every job or at least more than your competitors are able to assemble.

Who are the South Polers? These are people with enough academic intelligence to be in the game, but beyond that they thrive off their business savvy. They all have relatively high IQs but so do the North Polers who end up working for them. In the case of South Polers, their IQ is their ante—it gets them into the game. However, South Polers also have the magic. They almost instinctively know when to maneuver at just the right moments. They *envision* the next great product or service innovation, often doing so every day. They actually *execute* plans and put vision into action at the expense of competitors. Meanwhile, many of their more academic colleagues are analyzing, meeting, and considering what to do.

ACADEMIC BRILLIANCE MAY HAVE LITTLE TO DO WITH BUSINESS SAVVY

Academic success does not predict the success we are seeking in business. Yet, there are North Polers who exhibit what I call South Pole tendencies. I'm not advocating that South Polers rule over North Polers. To the contrary, I am pointing out that South Polers are every bit as valuable as their North Pole counterparts. In the examples that follow, Anthony Blumberg is an example of a North Poler, while Bob Stellato and Mike Hoffman are true South Polers. But, all of their successes stemmed not from their academic brilliance but from the magic they were able to put to work (their South Pole traits). The common thread among winners is that they *take action, take risk,* and *persuade others to believe.* These behaviors are not tied to academic brilliance—indeed, sometimes the attributes of academic achievers get in the way of these behaviors.

Take Action—Just Do It!

What a great, simple call to action. This attitude is behind almost every South and North Pole business success. I watched (and helped) Anthony Blumberg and his colleagues build a global emerging markets securities trading business at two different companies before he reached the age of 40 while others were simply *talking* about the difficulties of such a challenge. His businesses, built within very small brokerage companies, had no right to even get started. Why did they succeed, consistently being ranked alongside mega-firms like Morgan Stanley and Merrill Lynch? It is because Anthony just did it. He took action: He got on planes, called on customers, persuaded people to believe, and simply made it happen. While others were *weighing the possibilities* and staring at all the obstacles, Anthony just did it. He and his partners ultimately scaled the business and branded it *G-Trade*— a world leader in stock trading systems. He graduated from college in South Africa near the top of the class, but quickly morphed into a de facto South Poler. He came to the United States in the mid-1980s with $2,000 in his pocket and no local family or friends to rely on. He took a room in a three-bedroom apartment on the Lower East Side of Manhattan. He talked his way into a job in the trading pit at the New York Mercantile Exchange among a noted group of highly animated, hard-charging commodities traders—mostly of Italian American origin—and quickly assimilated. You can bet they paid little attention to his GPA. They adopted him, having him to their homes for holiday dinners. From there, he went to Citibank and learned about global equity trading, but left there to try his hand at building a business and the rest is history. Anthony is a winner. He has both North Pole academic achievement and South Pole savvy. A North Poler with South Pole magic—the most coveted talent mixture.

When looking for winning talent, look for people who have a bias for action and just do it. We've all seen this in successful

North Polers. The secret to the talent shortage is to find the South Polers who fit the bill.

Take the Risk

For a decade at Goldman Sachs and on Wall Street, when it came to Nasdaq trading, my friend Bob Stellato was clearly the man. Now the successful cofounder of Soleil Securities, Bob epitomizes the attributes of a savvy, street-smart, overachiever. He and I were having lunch recently and he amplified a clear attribute behind my smart-is-not-enough premise. He said, "I can't tell you how the EU and other modern economies will remain competitive, but I'll tell you what will keep America great in the face of global competition: We are *risk takers;* our country was built on that. Americans are a people who left their homelands to come here in the face of high risks. It's in our DNA. That will keep us competitive." Bob put his money and career where his mouth is. In 2002, in the wake of major restructuring on Wall Street, Bob launched a new business that offered services in a very new way. His company Soleil Securities has pushed forward a new paradigm. He has weathered the challenges, raised capital, and may have produced the industry's new winning business model. The company generates millions of dollars in revenue and has a list of blue-chip customers who were convinced Bob's business had what they needed. When looking for winning talent, look for risk takers. We've all seen this in North Poler success stories, but the secret to the talent shortage is to find the South Polers who fit the bill—both smart and savvy.

Persuade Others to Believe

When I think about Mike Hoffman, I see a vision of endless energy. A few years ago, my friend Andrea Cattani told me that

Mike was raising capital to fund his business, so I put my money where my mouth was. I invested over the phone without even looking at the business plan. I knew if Mike was behind the business it would all work out even though he had never built a business before. In less than 18 months, he returned the investment—up 50 percent. Mike founded Michael Hoffman Associates and then morphed it into "Changing Our World, Inc" to reflect the goal he had for his business—simply to change the world. No one ever accused Mike of thinking small. He built a great business and sold it to Omnicom, but not before evangelizing all those he encountered. Mike's company provided services to charities, not-for-profits, foundations, and companies involved in philanthropy. He often said, "I want to make a career in the field of philanthropy as prestigious as a career in investment banking. I want to attract the best and brightest to this field." He did; and he still does. When Mike's company had less than $3 million in revenue, he had a former chairman and CEO of Philip Morris on his board, attending every meeting and advising Mike as a mentor. Is it unheard of for such a small company to have someone of such stature as an active board member? No, it is just uncommon. When looking for winning talent, look for people who can evangelize others toward a passionate cause and inspire them to *believe*. These South Pole behaviors are nothing new in the annals of success.

AN EARLY SOUTH POLE CASE STUDY

South Polers have been around for a long time—historical examples prove it. In the early years, craftspeople and farmers were the core of our business economy. There are few examples of large commercial enterprises. Military units were much larger than most commercial enterprises. Therefore, military leaders were at the top of the food chain and serve as interesting historical examples from which to explore the South Pole phenomenon.

So imagine this. You're the CEO of a concern that's been in operation for about, oh, four score and seven years. You've only had the job a few years, but from day one the whole house of cards has been ripping apart underneath you. You need to hire someone to help you put your divided house back together. Your name is Abraham Lincoln and you've been fighting the Civil War for several years already. You've tried one top general after another and none has performed very well. McClelland and all those other mutton-chopped top-flight West Point graduates make a good case when they tell you how they're going to win this war and why the South just hasn't got enough manpower, factories, or money to put up much of a fight. There is just one small problem: The South seems to have all the talent, given the early course of the war. Those other West Point graduates, Robert E. Lee and Stonewall Jackson, are running circles around their classmates in the Union Army.

This is indeed particularly frustrating to you, because it is only talent that has essentially kept the South in business so far. On paper, the North should win this one, but talent is a very crucial factor in any business. All the other resources in the world can be nullified by it. And General Robert E. Lee is possibly one of the most brilliant academic graduates of the U.S. Military Academy at West Point. He graduated second in his class, and he only went into the military because his noble Virginia family couldn't afford to send him to college otherwise. General Lee may be the most talented military man in the nation and has been so for a couple of decades. He's like Alexander the Great with the brain of Aristotle—he has savvy and academic brilliance in ample supply. He would have been the logical choice for first in command if only Virginia hadn't decided to join the Confederacy and Lee hadn't decided to side with his state over his country. But he was lost to the competition. Top talent like him seems scarce. What are you to do, surrender? No, you look to the South Pole.

You're Abe Lincoln. You're fairly book smart yourself. You know there is no way you are going to find a general who's going to purely outsmart Robert E. Lee. But you also realize that you don't need an academic genius. You just need a reasonably smart man who can do the job, work his butt off for you, slog it out in the trenches, and who has a knack for finding a way to win. You need someone who is willing to win the war of attrition for you. If General Lee is Muhammad Ali, dancing around you and stinging like a bee, you need a Joltin' Joe Frasier who will stand toe-to-toe with him, know when to "zig and zag," take the abuse, outlast his opponent, and be smart enough to develop a winning strategy.

So you hear about this guy who's been running the volunteer army for you. At the start of the war, he's not even in the military. He's working as a clerk at his father's store in the Midwest someplace. He had graduated West Point in the bottom third of his class and went on to have a pretty undistinguished military career for a few years before working for his dad. On paper, Hiram is just about the last guy you'd hire. But a funny thing happened when he got that new commission with the volunteer army. He started winning and won the North's first real victory in the war. All the other brilliant, top generals say, "You can't be serious about promoting Grant. He's a loser, for god's sake. Come on, we're fighting a war to preserve the dang country here!"

But you, Lincoln, sense *something* about Grant—some sort of savvy. And you really like that Grant fights. He gets the job done. Too many of the other generals are maneuvering, retreating, and playing the waiting game. Grant is attacking. He's slogging through the bloody mess because he knows it's the only way to get it over with. So you go with your gut instinct and appoint Ulysses S. Grant (the name he was given mistakenly when his application to West Point was filled out for him) as the commander of the Union Army. And General Lee makes him look foolish at first, dancing around and outsmarting him—brilliant stuff, really. But Grant doesn't wait or play games. He advances. He executes. He splits the Confederacy in two, and he pounds and pounds and pounds the Southern forces into submission by making them fight, expending what few resources they have left. He knows instinctively how to beat the competition. Grant pummels Lee's forces while he sends William T. Sherman through Georgia, wreaking hell on earth, but finally forcing the war to an end. Grant gets the job done. It isn't pretty, but he has the talent to get the job done—in spite of his GPA.

The academic generals probably went back to teach at West Point and point out all the dumb, wasteful things Grant did to win the war. It wasn't elegant, but it worked. He deserved very low style points, but very high results points. The odd thing was that one of Grant's greatest admirers in the U.S. military was Robert E. Lee. General Lee was probably the only guy smart enough (other than Lincoln) to realize that Grant was just the right guy to beat him. Academic brilliance, in other words, isn't the most important measure of potential success. Sometimes success just takes sheer hard work, getting your hands dirty, and having the *savvy* to know intuitively what to do. Success takes the perseverance to stay the course, the judgment to modify the course, the communication skills to sell the plan, and the savvy to execute. None of which are classically measured by a person's college GPA.

In many ways, the military challenges faced by Lincoln as CEO are analogous to the war that U.S. businesses will wage with global competitors in this century. We *should* win if you look at our current platform, but the competition will surprise many. American CEOs will need to hire from the South Pole as part of their talent strategy. For too long, we have focused on academic achievement and IQ as a measure of a person's likelihood of succeeding. We have ignored the South Pole. No longer can we afford to do so—talent of the twenty-first century will be in short supply in comparison to demand. We must mine the South Pole as part of a complete talent management strategy. We can no longer leave this talent behind to rise solely by the hand of Adam Smith.

South Polers Have Emerged Despite the Companies They Worked For

Adam Smith's invisible hand is at work when these academic underachievers rise in the ranks. In the past, thanks to our free market and competition, these people found career growth, but it was typically done slogging through the ranks, rather than on a glide path of the company's management development program. Those programs are reserved for the high GPAs. Imagine if some of these people were hired into the company's elite entry-level training positions rather than into the call-center or the collections department jobs that are reserved for those who graduated with the less-than-impressive GPAs or from less-than-impressive colleges.

The secret source of superstar talent that can help us plug the hole in our talent pool are those who have graduated in the bottom half of their college classes. These people have the mix of intelligence and savvy to drive innovation, stand up to challenges, and ensure business success. Until now, conventional wisdom has been to hire the smartest (highest GPAs) for the sake of the company's future. Put them into training programs (usually poorly funded) and watch them grow into success stories. This works okay—but okay won't cut it going forward. You need amazing, not okay.

This brings me to those folks who bounce along with grades that put them in the lower half of the class. Often even at the absolute bottom of the class. Some have never even graduated at all, yet they have valedictorians working for them. Michael Dell is a fabulous example. I love the television commercial when he introduces himself and explains that, with his company's success, his parents have finally stopped worrying about the fact that he dropped out of college. Look at Tom Perna—from a leadership perspective he almost single-handedly put The Bank of New York on the map as a world leader in securities processing. He did this on Wall Street without a college degree—not a significant feat for someone in the early-1900s, except that Tom did it in the late 1980s. When Tom joined The Bank of New York, he was already a proven competitor, running Fidata, Inc. at the age of 30-something. Indeed, years earlier, he would not have been hired into the Bank's management training program. Imagine if he had been. What if his talent was somehow recognized as an entry-level candidate. Perhaps the bank would have suffered a few less painful blows in its securities processing sector. Tom emerged from the South Pole—then his talent was easily recognized.

How about Jamie Gioia? General Electric (GE) hired him after he graduated from mighty Southern Connecticut State College in 1981—although Southern is in Connecticut, it's not exactly Yale University by reputation. Did GE bring him into the elite management training program? No, they hired him as a collector in the credit department. He now runs the multibillion dollar vendor finance business for U.S. Bancorp at the age of 46. He recently took the job, but not before rising through the ranks of GE on his own merits and savvy. Before leaving GE, Jamie ran their healthcare vendor finance unit, regularly meeting with CEOs of *Fortune* 100 companies in the technology and healthcare sectors. Imagine what he could have done if he had been hired into the management training program at GE instead of slogging his way up the ranks the hard way.

To GE's credit, they have found a way to grow this type of talent once it is identified, which I explain more about later. This pool of talent is truly amazing. What makes these people tick? How do you find them and get them to work for you?

First, you need to decide to go looking for them. Then you need to look beyond academic credentials. GPAs are not meaningless, but GPA tells less than half the story when it comes to picking talent. In every pool of academic underachievers, there is a rough diamond that can be seen if you know what to look for. Put into the proper setting, it will quickly shine.

And so I encourage you to go to the South Pole to recruit your leadership team and the next generation of talent hired into your organization. If you don't, you may find that your competitors have. It will be apparent just about the time your market capitalization tanks because your company was out-savvied by the competition.

WHY IS THE GOAT A WINNER?

The U.S. Military Academy at West Point, has been around for a long time. It was the site of an important fort during the Revolutionary War, when Benedict Arnold tried to hand it over to the British. The first graduating class in 1807 had two students in it. Over the years, West Point has built up many quaint customs, as is done at most enduring institutions, including that of the "Goat."

It's graduation day at West Point, and a very happy cadet is awaiting his (or her) turn in line to receive his West Point diploma. To his chagrin, he is the Goat. This title challenged him dearly but it will serve him well in future years. The Goat is the lowest academically ranked cadet in the West Point graduating class—the last person in the class. To many, he is the object of "dumb" jokes; to me, he is a hero—a winner. Why? He is the last person in the class to survive West Point's merciless academic attrition—all the others flunked out. He is the *one* who found a way to graduate in the face of torturous challenge. He is last in the class, but the *first* one to prevail. He's found a way to win.

The Goat of the graduating class gets a special honor. After receiving his diploma, he gets a rousing cheer from the other cadets. He also receives, traditionally, a dollar from each classmate. This may sound condescending, but it really isn't. There certainly is some relief on the part of the other cadets that they are not the Goat. It's not the position that anyone strives for— quite the contrary. But the admiration the other cadets have for the Goat is very real. After all, they're the only other ones who know how tough it is to make it through West Point. Hundreds of other cadets have dropped out or been forced out, so the Goat is far from the lowest performer in the original class. He's just the last one who made it through the narrow gate.

Let's look at the Goat after graduation. There are less than desirable consequences to being the Goat of your West Point graduating class. In the old days, it meant you essentially had no choice about your military assignment. The top students in the class had their pick of a specialty. As the Goat, you were left with the last pickle in the bottom of the barrel—not that you weren't happy to get it. But your career in the military won't start out very brightly. You're going to have to prove yourself every day if you want to advance. The path is not going to be strewn with rose petals, but you've still got that chance. It's up to you. You're going to need to take action, take risks, and be persuasive.

The qualities of persistence, hard work, and ambition that allow the Goat to hang on and graduate are the very ones that have allowed a number of cadets near the bottom of their classes to excel. The military is very grade conscious, but it also rewards success and hard work. The West Point mascot isn't an owl but a mule—the lowest, hardest working animal in the barn. The mule is stubborn, strong, and industrious. These qualities are every bit as important as brains in succeeding in life—and in business. Just ask Generals Lee and Grant. For that matter, ask Condoleezza Rice, Jack Welch, or Lou Gerstner—I suspect they would agree.

Some of West Point's South Polers include renowned CEOs like a fellow named Jim Kimsey, the founder of America Online, and a list of others that would shock you. South Pole talent is no myth; it's just rarely cultivated by large corporate organizations. If we looked at Harvard, UMass, and "U" Name It, we would find countless examples of South Polers who became amazing business successes.

Joe Velli is another Bank of New York success story. As the chairman of one of the largest agency brokerage firms in the world, Joe is looking pretty smart—I'm sure colleges would love to have him speak to their MBA students. (It took him six years to complete his MBA.) The same colleges probably taught him the phrase "don't call us; we'll call you" in his earlier years as a college applicant. Joe is another South Poler who was not hired into a prestigious management training program. But 20 years after joining the bank, he leads a business that is perfectly positioned to answer the needs of his customers. The line of businesses he has put together through acquisitions and organic growth has virtually filled every need his customers' might have for an "end-to-end" solution. To top it off, he recently engineered a complicated "spin-off" that took his business division private, in partnership with the bank he formerly worked for. Thus, another South Poler rises through sheer force of will. What could possibly explain the South Pole phenomenon? How do these less than scholarly people rise above their academic superiors with such frequency?

Sometimes, hiring the Goat, as President Lincoln found out, is just the thing you need to do. People with this savvy— the ability to find a way to win—are precious in business. To achieve against great odds makes them winners. For the sake of our future, we need to find this talent early and cultivate it in better-funded, practical training programs. Although North Polers can also possess these characteristics, South Polers have them in abundance. The Box that follows contains a short list of South Pole talent with some familiar names.

- *Barbara Corcoran (1949–):* Although she coped with dyslexia, had difficulty reading, and didn't perform well in school, Corcoran managed to start a real estate company with a $1,000 loan and over 25 years developed it into a multi-billion dollar business.
- *Leo Tolstoy (1828–1910):* The author of War and Peace, he is celebrated as one of the world's greatest novelists. He attended university but was a poor student and did not graduate.*
- *John D. Rockefeller (1839–1937):* He only spent three months in college, but went on to build the Standard Oil Company into one of the largest and most profitable companies in the world at that time.*
- *Joe Velli (1957–):* He barely got by in high school and had a middling GPA in college, but Velli went on to become one of the youngest executive vice president ever at The Bank of New York and became Chairman and CEO of its Securities Group, and created the world's largest agency brokerage at a time when others in his industry had trouble seeing beyond the next 24 hours.

- *David Neeleman (1959–):* A college dropout with ADD who cares about his employees, he keeps America flying high as CEO of the innovative low-cost airline, JetBlue.*

- *Bob Parsons (1950–):* He wasn't much of a student and received poor grades in high school but didn't let that stop him from becoming founder and CEO of Parsons Technology (which sold for $64 million) and more recently, Go Daddy, the world's largest domain name registrar.*

- *Wayne Huizenga (1937–):* A college dropout, he is known for his Midas touch in business and founded three Fortune 500 companies, including Blockbuster Video.*

- *Masatoshi Koshiba (1926–):* He was the worst student in his class at the University of Tokyo but later went on to win the Nobel Prize in Physics in 2002 for pioneering contributions to the field of astrophysics.*

- *Erin Brockovich (1960–):* The subject of the hit movie, she had such difficulties in school that she was told she'd probably never make it to college; however, Brokovich achieved fame and fortune after uncovering the contamination of drinking water by a utilities giant and helping win the largest toxic tort injury settlement ($333M) in U.S. history.*

- *Peter Jennings (1938–2005):* Despite dropping out of high school, he brought world leaders to heel as anchor and senior editor of ABC's *World News Tonight.*

- *Richard Branson (1950–):* British billionaire and owner of Virgin, he was dyslexic and quit school at the age of 16.*

*Autodidactic Profiles: Self-educated People Who've Made a Difference http://www.autodidactic.com/profiles/profiles.htm

When was the last time you hired someone like this? There are people like this in every business talent pool. They are often overlooked in the early hiring process, but among them are stars of the future. The problem is that these people typically succeed with little assistance from the organization that hired them. We can't afford to continue this highly inefficient approach to talent selection and development. We need to hire *all* the great talent that is graduating, not just those we can easily select from GPA ranking. Many of those students with high GPAs will eventually work for the Barbara Corcorans, Tom Pernas, or the Jamie Gioias of the world. Typically these people become key leaders who find a way to drive their teams to success. They understand that if *the team fails, the leader fails; and the game is over.*

4

☆☆ Emotional ☆☆ Intelligence Is More Important Than Grade Point Average

To wear your heart on your sleeve isn't a very good plan; you should wear it inside, where it functions best.

—Margaret Thatcher

Isn't Emotional Intelligence an Oxymoron like Military Intelligence?

Aren't emotions and intelligence supposed to be opposites? Haven't we always been taught that when we get emotional we're acting stupidly? Isn't the ideal businessperson still the calm, rational thinker? Well, yes and no. Part of the problem is that the term *emotional* has become a pejorative term, a negative. No one wants to be seen as emotional—except maybe a daytime talk-show host or two. When people talk about emotional intelligence (EI) these days, they're not talking about being at the mercy of our emotions but, quite the contrary, being in control of our emotions, using them productively and creatively. Since the dawn of the Enlightened Age, we have valued using our cognitive abilities to help us learn and get ahead in life. Wikipedia explains, "The expression emotional intelligence or EI indicates a kind of intelligence or skill that involves the ability to perceive, assess and positively influence one's own and other people's emotions."[1] Some of our scholarly friends from the North Pole lack this sort of intangible, hard-to-measure talent (i.e., there is no EI curriculum and hence, no GPA to rank students for their EI prowess).

But why is EI such a hot-button issue now? And is it just the latest in a long line of impractical, academic business theories and get-rich-quick business fads? There are two main reasons why EI is such a buzz word in today's business environment. The first is a former *New York Times* science writer and Harvard professor Daniel Goleman who has written two recent influential books on the topic: *Emotional Intelligence* in 1995 and *Working with Emotional Intelligence* in 1998. The second reason is that (in case I still have not made this clear enough) the world has changed dramatically, and the business world no less than any other sector. Productivity is key and EI is a key to productivity. According to the Institute for Health and Human Potential,[2] if you were to check the figures on corporate productivity you would learn that:

- In jobs of medium complexity (sales clerks, mechanics), a top performer is 12 times more productive than those at the bottom and 85 percent more productive than an average performer.
- In the most complex jobs (insurance salespeople, account managers), a top performer is 127 percent more productive than an average performer.
- Competency research in over 200 companies and organizations worldwide suggests that about one-third of this difference is due to technical skill and cognitive ability while *two-thirds is due to emotional competence.* (In top leadership positions, over four-fifths of the difference is due to emotional competence.)

Ah, the Bad Ol' Days

To dramatize the evolution of people-to-people dealings, I want you to consider this: A thousand years ago, the only emotion you needed to succeed in the world was hostility. You assembled an army from your local fiefdoms and went to slaughter and pillage your nearest neighbor. An executive in medieval days didn't really have to know how to get along with people, he really only needed to know the best way to lop their heads off with a pole-axe. This business model endured in one form or another for a considerably long time—maybe until about the time of the atomic bomb tests at Alamagordo, New Mexico. Suddenly, thanks to something called *mutually assured destruction,* blowing up your neighbor wasn't so practical anymore. You were now going to have to get along if you wanted his or her treasure. Strangely, this method proved to be even more profitable, when done correctly, than the old slash-and-burn tactics. People realized they could actually help each other get richer, instead of just getting rich at the other person's expense.

If you think heavy-handed business tactics are strictly a thing of the distant past, then consider a couple of not-so-long-ago cases. Henry Clay Frick, one of the stars of the Gilded Age (there is a museum named after him in Manhattan, too), hired a private militia of three hundred Pinkerton guards and had them fire into a crowd of his steel workers and their families when they were on strike. And none other than Henry Ford Sr. had a secret police force of his own to spy on his plant workers, and is said to have kept machine guns, tear gas, and a private army at hand in the event of trouble arising from union organizers.

You're probably not going to get away with business tactics like that in the United States anymore. Henry Ford is in so many ways the classic American business entrepreneur model. Through sheer industry, aggression, and much technical know-how, he built one of the largest corporations in the world, after starting off with an old horse buggy in his garage. He invented the assembly line, and he was smart enough to realize that he needed people with enough money to buy his automobiles, so he paid his workers a handsome salary for the time. The pluck and ingenuity Ford exhibited and exemplified are still valuable business attributes. They will undoubtedly never go out of fashion. It is interesting to compare Ford to another self-made business mogul of a more recent vintage—Michael Dell.

Michael Dell was just an okay student hoping to become a doctor before he dropped out of his college in Texas in the mid-1980s. But, like Ford, he liked to tinker with mechanical things. Specifically, he liked to build his own computers from scratch. It certainly cost less than buying them retail. (In 1984, a brand new Macintosh cost about $2,000 and had about the same computing power as a bottom-of-the-line digital camera today.) Like Ford, Dell had a great idea to make his business more efficient and profitable—selling directly to customers, and building each computer, in effect, as a custom model after he got the order. It was like Burger King's "Have it your way" applied to micro-circuitry. Fast-forward 20 years and Dell Computers is the largest computer supplier in the world and still operating more or less on Michael Dell's original have-it-your-way concept. But there is one big difference between Michael Dell and his entrepreneurial forebear Henry Ford. Dell could not afford to be mean to his employees. Michael Dell probably isn't the type who likes being mean to anyone, but if he had been, his company in the late twentieth century almost certainly would not have succeeded. And it's not only because we value getting along with each other these days but also because of a thing called communications—the very thing that has been changing the world so dramatically for the past century. One of the fundamental precepts of EI rests with a person's ability to control or manage his or her emotions, driving positive outcomes.

THE FUTURE IS UPON US

Like it or not we are now living in, and even far beyond, Orwell's world of *1984* (ironically enough, the year Dell started his home-grown company). We live in a world rife with cell phones, laptops, BlackBerrys, 24-hour cable news, Internet blogs, and you name it. Whatever you do these days, especially in the business world, is going to be commented on—and possibly even recorded for posterity with a cell-phone camera by someone. And that news, if it's juicy enough, can be broadcast to the entire world 10 seconds later. The behavior of individual managers is under a microscope for all the world to see.

I'm not saying there aren't still dictatorial bosses out there. Steve Jobs can still get away with calling an employee a "bozo" and not get canned by his board. Michael Eisner, however, wasn't so lucky. Jobs still has a relatively self-contained corporate fiefdom to himself out there in Cupertino, California, and is more of a celebrity than a business executive. His little tantrums—throwing nonfunctioning products off the stage during presentations, for instance—really just add to the Apple mystique. His creativity has Apple rolling along nicely.

Communications today is everything. How many manufacturing jobs are even left in the United States? Ford's Red River facility is still there in Detroit, but for how much longer? It only follows then that those business executives who are masters at communicating are the new stars. And how do you become expert at communicating with people? Is it by studying huge technical tomes? No, it is by gaining mastery of your emotions— learning to wield not just your cognitive intelligence but also your EI or practical intelligence. Barbara Corcoran explained her knack for communicating by telling me she actually "visualizes" concepts and plans; "I can see them" she said. Because of this, she can explain her ideas in graphic ways that allow others to "see" what she is saying. As a South Poler, with a consistent D average, she was more likely to speak than write. Except, of course, for creative writing where she excelled.

But what about good old duplicity, you ask? Why isn't it still okay just to act friendly to people while you're sticking a knife in their backs? Beyond the obvious moral and ethical reasons, it's because in this day of communications it's bound to come out. Remember those glossy ads of Leona Helmsley in the margins of the *New Yorker* with the title "Be a guest of the Queen," or whatever they were trying to foist off on people? After she was exposed as a gorgon to her employees, those ads looked comical. Today, you can't afford to be found out. Learning to be sincere is part of EI. Is it really going to turn out that honesty is the best policy after all? Incredible as it seems, yes it is.

Emotional Intelligence Emerges from—The Lab?

This notion of EI is not entirely new. It's really just become painfully crucial in the modern business world. Back in 1940, David Wechsler (the creator of a popular IQ test) started talking about "nonintellective" (i.e., emotional) as different from "intellective" elements in the brain. Wechsler himself was not the most suave of communicators, being more of the deep-thinking college professor type. He thought of intelligence not as just being good at filling out IQ tests but as the "aggregate" or global "capacity" of people to act consciously, and specifically, to deal with their environment. Long before Daniel Goleman, Wechsler was saying that these nonintellective or emotional qualities were necessary for success in life.

In 1983, Howard Gardner (a professor at Harvard) started talking about *multiple intelligences.* According to him, "intrapersonal" and "interpersonal intelligences" are as important as cognitive skills. The IQ test people are measuring cognitive skills when they ask you to pick out which item in a group of five doesn't belong. Just for fun, some television interviewer should ask Jack Welch (former CEO of GE), if he knows how long it will take Johnny to get from Point A to Point C by way of Point B if Points A and B are equidistant from Point C and the distance from Point A to Point C is 3.2 miles and Johnny is rid-ing his bicycle at 6.5 miles per hour. Welch would probably smile and give the correct answer, which is "What the hell does that have to do with business?"

About 1990, two professors, Peter Salovey and John Mayer, used the term *emotional intelligence.* For them, EI was "a form of social intelligence that involves the ability to monitor one's own and others feelings and emotions, to discriminate among them, and to use this information to guide one's thinking and action."[3]

Listening to Salovey and Mayer, it's easy to see why this movement didn't really kick off until Goleman wrote his first book in 1995. The irony is that the scholars who explored the theory before him were just not that good at communicating their ideas. They were old-school IQ guys. Do the research, write the report in as obscure a manner as you possibly can (so that only other academic scholars will have even the vaguest idea of just what you are talking about), then wait for the Nobel Prize committee to spring into action on your behalf—50 years later.

Sometime in the mid-1990s, Daniel Goleman, a psychologist and professor at Harvard, wrote what was to become the seminal work of the new EI era, *Emotional Intelligence.* The small fact that it also became a best seller probably produced a few academic snickers up in Cambridge, but it proved that Goleman was a master of communication. He's the one who finally allowed us less fortunate mortals to "get it." It was not, really, his skills as a psychologist that were most important here, but his skills as a communicator, honed by years of writing for the *New York Times.*

Probably the most important point of his new book is that EI is not only measurable, but capable of being improved. When Isaac Newton published *Principa Mathematica,* there weren't too many readers out there picking up a copy and thinking (i.e., cogitating) to themselves, "Oh, yeah. I see. I can do that." As wonderful as the new science of calculus was, and is, it's not really going to help you land that account with Starbucks.

Goleman's work was indeed groundbreaking. Especially when three years later, he came out with *Working with Emotional Intelligence,* which applied his ideas directly to the business world.[4] The earlier book was more about theory and using the techniques in general education. I discuss his findings in greater detail later, as well as explain why I think that the best combinations of IQ and EI occur at both the North and South Pole of the competent talent pool spectrum. North Polers obviously are rich in IQ, but it tends to be South Polers who, while no dummies, are particularly rich in EI. South Polers, unlike the pampered academic elites, have had to struggle to gain a foothold and to learn ways other than just wowing everyone with their test results to get ahead. If you've never experienced the stress of having to pass the final exam to indeed pass the course, you've never struggled academically and walked in the shoes of the South Poler.

In the early twentieth century, a book was published that offered the following now rather familiar-sounding advice about how to be a leader in business. This book, which was a best seller and had nothing to do with academic achievement, espoused that a leader's job often includes changing people's attitudes and behavior. Some suggestions to accomplish this include:

1. Begin with praise and honest appreciation.
2. Call attention to people's mistakes indirectly.
3. Talk about your own mistakes before criticizing the other person.
4. Ask questions instead of giving direct orders.
5. Let the other person save face.

6. Praise the slightest improvement and praise every improvement. Be "hearty in your approbation and lavish in your praise."

7. Give the other person a fine reputation to live up to.

8. Use encouragement. Make the fault seem easy to correct.

9. Make the other person happy about doing the thing you suggest.

The writer's name was Dale Carnegie, and his book, *How to Win Friends and Influence People,*[5] sold more than a few copies. Not much of his information was entirely new, but it put the concept of EI in layperson's terms. People have always known, at least instinctively, that being in control of our emotions is important—to stay out of jail if for no other reason. The difference these days is, first, that scientists like Goleman and the others are learning practical, measurable means of assessing, applying, and teaching these skills so that the emotional quotient is recognized as more than just some magic that a person is born with. At long last, they're turning EI into a science. Second, in a world dominated by communications, such skills have never been more important for financial and personal success.

If you'd like to have a good, up-to-date, concrete example of the importance of communication skills in business success compared to sheer inventiveness, just think about the last piece of software you purchased. This thing is brilliant. It's going to change your life. The programmers who wrote this code are geniuses, pure and simple. Then you open the instruction manual. Huh? Enough with the graphs and pie charts already—just tell me which disc I'm supposed to put in first. The greatest, noblest ideas in the world are worthless if they cannot be conveyed to other people. The brilliant inventor deserves all the credit in the world, but he or she alone cannot (in most cases) capitalize on his or her work. It almost always takes another genius to do that—the brilliant marketer.

This brings us back to the colorful example of Steve Jobs at Apple Computer. Jobs is not the guy in the lab calibrating the densitometers. He's up front making the most of the great work of his tech guys. The conclusion is apparent. Scholarly achievers have no patent on the savvy that comes from having practical intelligence, EI, or Wechsler's nonintellect. Indeed, many lack the savvy needed to compete with South Polers.

And there you have it. That's the reason you'll find many valedictorians working for those with less academic prowess. South Polers have strong EI levels that give them the tools to be winners. They are empathetic. They can read people. They can visualize concepts and clearly articulate them. Find them for your team and give them room to fly. Do you need more evidence? Read on and remember when *the team fails, the leader fails; and the game is over.*

5

☆ ☆ Five South Pole ☆ ☆ Talent Secrets

Never doubt that a small group of committed people can change the world. Indeed it's the only thing that ever has.

—Anonymous

What Exactly Is the South Pole Theory?

The South Pole theory is of little value if you can't implement it. To do so, you need to be able to evaluate potential South Pole talent using behaviorial interview techniques that are explained later in the book. Initially, you need to decide which of these academic underachievers are potential South Polers.

South Polers are actually brilliant people with significant intellectual capacity and an extraordinary ability to find a way to get things done. I assert that they typically fit the following description when you evaluate their college or high school records:

- IQ above 120 (to the extent the IQ score is available).
- GPA below 3.0.
- A fairly high GPA in one subject (i.e., social science, languages) that is above 3.5 or at least .75 greater than their overall GPA—that is, if the GPA is 2.6, then the subject matter GPA would be 3.35 or greater. (They tend to achieve in areas that interest them.)
- A strong track record of extracurricular activities and leadership roles that kept them very busy, allowing less time to devote to academics.

- A measurable, significant, stand-out accomplishment—such as winner of a national essay contest, elected to a high office at programs like the American Legion's Boy's/Girl's State, winners in Odyssey of the Mind, and so on.

- Probably dyslexic or afflicted with some sort of learning disability; sometimes they are classified with a "504" designation in accordance with educational classification standards specified in federal legislation.

Although the theory is still evolving, we hope to offer software that will allow employers and individuals to enter candidate data and receive a "South Poler probability ranking." Our web site should offer this in the future. For now, you can begin approaching this manually by looking at the factors just listed. Beyond the data component, you will find that South Polers have at least five things in common when looking at broad attributes. I call these the Five Secrets.

Secret 1: They Are the Communicators

I will tell you one thing for sure about successful employees, managers, and executives. They're busy getting crucial feedback from all over but never forget what's most important: They *listen*. They communicate.

South Polers tend to be masters at communication. South Polers are smart people, usually with a wiring or priority-setting problem that holds them back in the world of academics. Yet, that is the world they play in for the first 18 (or more) years of their competitive lives. South Polers have to develop significant compensatory skills to stay afloat. Similar to blind people who develop keener senses of smell, hearing, and touch, South Polers become keen communicators. As a result, they may talk to their teachers to negotiate better grades, extensions, or extra credit. They make the case for acceptance into a club or a program reserved for those with better grades. They are persuasive.

I suspect that John H. Johnson was a South Poler who turned his great talent for communication into his business. He was born in rural Arkansas in 1918 into a poor family. His father, who was only one generation removed from slavery, died in a sawmill accident when Johnny was only eight years old. His mother supported the family for years and managed to save enough to move her family to Chicago, where Johnson finally got a chance to get a good public education. After that, there really was no stopping him. He briefly attended both the University of Chicago and Northwestern, but did not graduate. Eventually, Johnson grew up to be founder, publisher, chairman, and CEO of the Johnson Publishing Company of Chicago, Illinois. Johnson made communications his business. His company is not only the largest African American-owned publishing company in the world, producing such well-known magazines as *Ebony* and *Jet,* but it was also a pioneer in the publishing industry. Mr. Johnson died not too long ago at the age of 87 but the company he founded out of abject poverty (and undoubtedly in the face of brutal racism), now also has a book division with over two thousand employees and claims sales of almost $400 million. John H. Johnson was a great communicator, and the most important thing he communicated to America and the world is: You can't keep me down.

The next time you find yourself licking your wounds, whining about the bad hand fate has dealt you and how can you be expected to succeed against such odds, think about John H. Johnson. Ask yourself if you would have gotten up off the mat after that kind of start in life. South Polers do it all the time in varying degrees. They're accustomed to adversity. They don't whine and they embody Secret 2.

Secret 2: They Have Character Born of Suffering or Challenges

Some men give up their desires when they have almost reached the goal; while others on the contrary obtain a victory by exerting at the last moment, more vigorous efforts than before.

—Ploybius (BC 203–120)

Buddha is attributed with the following quote; "Endurance is one of the most difficult disciplines, but it is to the one who endures that the final victory comes." Suffering builds winners. The people you are seeking will have endured some character-building challenges. For some, it was being the first-generation child of an immigrant that forced them to be self-sufficient. For others, it was difficulty earning good grades or finding it difficult to fit in with certain groups. For still others, it was physical adversity or poverty.

Take this story for example. I bet you've never heard of Paul Orfalea.

In his book, Paul Orfalea said that his early work experiences led him to believe he was totally unemployable. Paul certainly epitomizes the classic South Poler—massively dyslexic, he never tested well and suffered through school and college. Indeed, his teachers actually put him into special education classes. Why? He did not fit the classic mold of a student. This is often the case with South Polers. They have above average and sometimes genius levels of IQ but don't display it academically. They rank low in their classes and don't apply themselves to academic pursuits that don't appeal to them. Basically, they appear to be destined for less than stellar careers.

Had Paul Orfalea applied to Federal Express (FedEx) for their management training program when he finally graduated from college, he certainly would not have been hired. Several years later, if FedEx had had the vision to pursue the retail copy business and hire a headhunter to recruit a division head to launch the business with plans for thousands of offices supporting millions of customers, I doubt they would have hired Paul Orfalea, the manager of a few copy stores in California. Had they done so, they may have saved billions of dollars—they could have given this brilliant South Poler a platform that far surpassed the platform he used to launch his little copy business. How could they have saved billions? They could have hired Paul rather than buying his company once he successfully scaled it. Yes, FedEx bought Paul's business for more than $2,000,000,000. Yes, that's *$2 billion*. Paul's college classmate gave him a nickname, and Paul used it to name the company he started in a small copy stand in California. He called the business Kinko's. The founder of Kinko's who scaled the company to over 1,500 stores with state-of-the-art systems and close to 25,000 employees was a South Poler with red, kinky hair named Paul Orfalea.

Paul felt the pain felt by many who are not top academic achievers. In the introduction of his book, he writes: "I graduated from high school, with a focus on woodshop, eighth from the bottom of my class of 1,200. Frankly, I still have no idea how those seven kids managed to do worse than I did."[1]

He was made to believe by most that he would never amount to anything. But Paul's mother was a great supporter. In his book, he writes that she said, "You know, Paul, the A students work for the B students, the C students run the companies, and the D students dedicate the buildings."[2]

Now that's encouragement. Do you think any of Paul's professors in college ever told him that? No, they probably told him to go back to the woodshop. And you know what? If a guy with the right stuff like Paul Orfalea did put his all into woodshop, he'd probably become either a great cabinet maker or invent some revolutionary new way to construct houses. South Polers make what they have work, often with spectacular results, because they've usually learned one of the great lessons of all—it's a waste of time to feel sorry for yourself.

Stories like Paul's have been made for years and on scales large and small. There is the little-known but remarkable story of Godel Wroblewski. Who is Godel Wroblewski? In the grand scheme of things, he's probably not that great a figure. But what he accomplished was indeed great. If the corporate food giant Tyson wanted to get into the kosher chicken business in Australia, then maybe there would be another story about the billion dollar acquisition of a South Poler's business. In his biography, *My Battle for Survival from Mlyny to Melbourne,* he relates the rather incredible and heart-rending tale of how he was raised in a dirt-poor Polish farming community and then lost his entire family during the Holocaust. He himself became a prisoner at Buchenwald and Schlieben and was later liberated from the camp at Theresienstadt.

During his internment, he contracted tuberculosis and was sent to a sanitarium in Switzerland for three years. Godel, however, was an ambitious, hard-working sort and he wasn't going to let these setbacks keep him from realizing his dreams. So he packed up and moved to Melbourne, Australia, to help his brother-in-law start up a kosher chicken business. It is to this day the best-known business of its kind in Australia. Nobody's ever going to be making any movies out of the life of Godel Wroby (he changed his name when he reached Melbourne), but nobody's going to stop him either. It's a strange thing about hardship. It ruins some people, but it makes others stronger. Obviously, you're looking for the latter kind of talent because you can count on trouble later on down the road.

General George Patton is credited with the statement, "There is no discipline, but perfect discipline." He should have said, "There is no discipline, but self-discipline." Most successful businesspeople are highly disciplined. They often look to themselves first when things don't go well. They are the first to blame themselves and take corrective action. This behavior stems from their character—that intangible "something" that people who find a way to win just happen to have. People of character have discipline, and they have typically suffered to get there. You can't test someone for discipline. When looking for people who have it, find out how they've suffered or been challenged. Ask the right questions and you'll see the character bubble up to the surface.

Secret 3: Somehow They've Stood Out

Certainly not as academic performers, but the people you seek have probably stood out in some way or in some area of pursuit and did so at an early age. The standout achievements may seem like insignificant childhood stories, but they were the precursor of a future of a string of small achievements that collectively add up. They may have starred in school plays, excelled in 4-H, or led the student council or the debate team, all the while underperforming academically. Or they simply were the ones that teachers saw as "operators"—perhaps they were wise beyond their years. Typically their peers looked up to them in some way, despite their academic mediocrity. Or sometimes these students were shunned from the popular circle of students. Maybe there was an unspoken jealousy or, subconsciously, they may have been seen as a threat. Typically, however, South Polers connect with all factions of the class—having connections with the popular crowd, the nerds, the motor-heads, and so on.

I can't resist telling this story as an illustration. It comes up as a favorite story at my family events on occasion. I'm a classic South Poler myself. I graduated in the bottom half of my class at West Point and indeed was only accepted to West Point because of some early leadership accomplishments that had nothing to do with academics. I was never really motivated to study. I was attracted to and distracted by other things. My grades, like those of all South Polers, were not an indication of what I could do. All the way back in third grade at Hayestown Elementary School in Danbury, Connecticut, I had the dubious distinction of being a champion marble player. The playground was my domain. Each day I would win dozens of marbles and often clean out my opponent's entire marble supply. Lots of kids win at marbles, so what? The uniqueness comes in because, at the age of nine, I decided to set up a business selling marbles. It was simple. I would win the marbles and sell them back to the other players in little plastic bags at a price that was below the local store price. I thought it was great. I was saving them money and turning a nice profit for myself. This went on for a few months until my mother asked me how I was getting all this pocket change. I was raised in a wonderful Italian American family with very sincere, homespun values. My business model appeared less than respectable to my mom. She made me repay all the money and give back any excess marble inventory I had not yet sold. Thankfully, I had some resilience or my mom may have thwarted my future entrepreneurial ambitions. To this day when my mom talks of my current business escapades, she invariably returns to the marble story. She insists it was a precursor of things to come for me. My sisters say they really don't know what their brother does for a living, but they are sure it has something to do with selling marbles. Anyway, you get the point.

Dave Shaffer, famous for his executive leadership as former COO of the Thomson Corporation and CEO of Thomson Financial, the tenacious competitor to Bloomberg and Reuters, is indeed a classic South Poler who stood out at an early age for his business acumen. This is another simple example, but you will learn that there are more of these stories than you may think if you begin to "pole" people. The middle child of his siblings, Dave was an industrious young boy in the Midwest. He tells the story of his enterprising youth this way: "As a boy I was always working—from the age of about seven in fact. My best business was mowing lawns." Lawn mowing is not all that unusual for most kids; however, unlike most kids, Dave was not satisfied with making a little pocket money. He had a hand-operated mower and quickly realized that a power mower would allow him to be more productive and mow more lawns. So, he saved his money, and when he had amassed enough capital, he bought a power mower and the rest is history. I bet he hired another kid to use the old mower and begin to scale the business. Had he not joined the navy, perhaps he would have become a lawn care mogul with a brand like ChemLawn. Suffice it to say he would have made a great entrepreneur. That, however, was not in the cards. Dave finished high school without the grades to win a college scholarship, so he joined the navy and served his country. When he was tested, the navy found him to be quite bright; despite his high school GPA. As a result, he was sent to language school where he excelled. He left the navy after three plus years and won an entry-level job in the corporate world. He then moved to Dun and Bradstreet where he excelled. The company said that if he wanted a corporate career, he needed to get a college degree. Because he was married with small children, that was not a possibility. To Dun and Bradstreet's credit, they found him a way into the graduate program at Northwestern University. So, the South Poler without a formal bachelor's degree earned his masters' degree while working full-time at his day job. Finishing his career at the Thomson Corporation, David has left his mark. As a member of the executive team, he has pulled together a company that scaled through disparate acquisitions to emerge as reengineered, profitable, efficient, well organized, and growing. But he first stood out by investing his capital in a power mower.

The bottom line is that South Polers, while underperforming academically, have somehow stood out somewhere. Maybe it was not academically or on the sports field (although many athletes have South Pole attributes), but in life—on the playground, in art class, in student government, or in the community. These may appear to be seemingly insignificant standout activities, and you may ask if I am really serious about selling marbles and mowing lawns. I am. Among our peers, we were doing the unusual—no matter how seemingly insignificant. And if you follow the progression of standout achievements, they continue to move to greater levels of significance.

Additionally, South Polers stand out to their peers. They find that both their more scholarly friends as well as those less studious ones always seem to seek them out for advice and support. Although not so at school, Barbara Corcoran ran the show in her neighborhood. As she matured, others sought her advice and counsel. It's amazing that South Polers all have stories of how they were the soothsayers or the confidants when it came to others seeking advice. Somehow these other folks— their peers—saw something special in them. I promise you that somewhere, early on and often, they stood out.

Secret 4: They Are Always Passionate

South Polers rarely take a minor stand. To them, every position they take is tied to an intense belief that will lead to winning. If they don't feel it, they don't act.

Tony Brown's story should be an inspiration to every aspiring young person. In the 1970s, Tony Brown was orphaned, raised by his aunt in Harlem with his younger siblings. While in junior high school, Tony achieved the grades he needed to "get out of Harlem and into a top-flight high school opportunity at Horace Mann" in the Bronx. Tony's passion and drive allowed him these early achievements. However, at Harvard, he was firmly planted in the South Pole—graduating in the bottom half of his class (the place where private equity firms, investment banks, and coveted corporate training programs tend not to look—even Harvard has a South Pole). He was overlooked by most who hired his higher-ranked classmates. The fact that he had to work part-time jobs while at Harvard to pay his tuition may somewhat explain his less-than-stellar academic performance.

Fortunately, after graduation and a stint in the medical products industry, he did find a job at Lehman Brothers, but not as a management trainee. They must have felt they were taking a chance on him when he was hired, but he quickly proved himself on the trading floor. That's the place where daring and risk-taking rule the day. He then made a career change to the executive search industry where he quickly earned credibility. In 2002, he made another shift into uncharted waters in the emerging world of corporate talent acquisition. Until recently, Tony led the talent acquisition unit at the Wall Street investment bank, Bear Stearns. Not only did he lead the group, he rebuilt the group, integrating the function into a formal service provider in the company, and *won* this unit a seat at the table with business heads who used to look at this human resource function as little more than a provider of administrative services.

Tony's passion toward his career comes through when he says: "I often reflect on whether I made the right decision to enter this [talent] aspect of the business . . ." He also says, "when I saw the growth plans at Bear, and saw the way we were eventually viewed by the business units at Bear, I knew this was a very good decision and a great career opportunity. The future demand for what I do will just continue to grow." Tony is passionate about what he does. He was constantly thinking about the business and hired a great team around him. If Tony did not believe that his team could provide the fuel that Bear Stearns needed to achieve its goals, he would not have done the job. His passion would not allow it.

Secret 5: They Will Always Be Creative

John Lennon wrote, "Some may say I'm a dreamer, but I'm not the only one." The fact is that our targeted pool of talent is made up of very creative minds. They will challenge conventional thinking. Indeed, they were born questioning. They question everything. As a result, they often find themselves in entrepreneurial positions. Their creativity stems from seeing everything as an opportunity for change. What better trait for an executive? Innovation and the ability to implement is what makes a business work.

In the *McKinsey Quarterly*, Erica J. Bever, Elizabeth Stephenson, and David W. Tanner discuss the views of a panel of executives this way:

> Almost 50 percent of the executives on the global panel believe that innovation—either the improvement of current products or the emergence of new ones—will be the most important driver of growth during the next five years.[3]

Inventor Dean Kamen, who provides evidence of the South Pole creativity characteristic, has been described this way:

> Electromechanical engineer, inventor, and entrepreneur Kamen didn't like school and earned poor grades while growing up, yet his inventions have changed lives. At the age of 24, he developed the first portable insulin pump, and some of his most recent inventions include an intravascular heart stent used to reduce blockage in arteries, and the Independence 3000 IBOT, an all-terrain wheelchair that can climb stairs and balance itself upright on two wheels. That technology also led to the production of the Segway Human Transportor, a two-wheeled battery-powered device that can travel up to eight miles per hour. Kamen also founded FIRST (For Inspiration and Recognition of Science and Technology), a nonprofit orga-

nization that motivates American children to learn about science and technology by pairing engineers and scientists with
students in a national robot-building competition[4]

It's the vision thing. It's thinking differently, to be sure.

Barbara Corcoran's is an amazing story. If I could ever identify a poster child for the classic South Poler, Barbara would be
it. A consistent D student, on her web site (www.barbaracorcoran
.com), she describes herself.

About Me

Barbara Corcoran's credentials include straight D's in
high school and college and twenty jobs by the time she
turned twenty-three. It was her next job, however, that
would make her one of the most successful entrepreneurs in the country, when she borrowed $1,000 from her
boyfriend and quit her job as a waitress to start a tiny real
estate company in New York City. Over the next twenty-
five years, she'd parlay that $1,000 loan into a $5 billion
real estate business.

Selecting South Polers is anything but an exact science.
They are a complicated lot who come in all shapes and sizes.
The things they have in common are academic underachieve-
ment, passion, creativity, and character bred of challenges;
they are great communicators and have stood out early and
often. They are high in EI as well as IQ. They can be found by
analyzing their performance history using behavior interview
techniques that I share with you in the coming chapters. You
need these people on your team.

You can find her described in various newspaper articles in
a very different way, such as the excerpt in the box that follows.

BIG DEAL: A Gun, a Gallop and a Goodbye*

By William Neuman

Barbara Corcoran, one of the matriarchs of New York real estate, has never seemed like the type to ride off into the sunset. But that is more or less what she did at her going-away party at Chelsea Piers this month, when she got on a white horse and rode away. After waving goodbye to the hundreds of brokers who came to the sendoff, she rode the horse out of sight and dismounted at a waiting car. . . . Ms. Corcoran, 56, started her company, the Corcoran Group, in 1973 and sold it to the real estate conglomerate NRT, an arm of the Cendant Corporation, in September 2001, for what she said was $66 million.

*New York Times, October 30, 2005.

I interviewed Barbara to get her perspective on my South Pole Theory. We discussed her experiences in school and at work in great detail. Here is a snapshot of how she matches up against the Five Secrets to South Pole Talent:

1. *Communicator:* She kiddingly calls it her ability to B.S. The fact is that building a sales empire of sorts takes a great communicator. She attributes her communication skills to her underlying ability to actually visualize ideas and thoughts. Then when she puts them into words, they are clear and allow others to visualize what she is saying, planning, or describing.

2. *Challenge/suffer:* She says she was convinced by second grade that she was not going to be able to read and it hurt. In third grade, she was sent back to second grade, which was devastating. Throughout her academic years she was given "charity Ds" so she would pass, or she attended summer school to get a passing grade. She noted

that her experiences created a great capacity for empathy, which translated into being a great people-person.

3. *Stood out:* Although she suffered academically, she was the neighborhood leader. Among peers who knew her outside of school, she was the boss they wanted to follow.

4. *Passionate:* She describes her passion as a deep need to know. As she said when I talked to her about this attribute, "The passion comes from a need to succeed and from a deep fear of failing." Although few people ever recognized it, she was constantly afraid she was going to fail.

5. *Creative:* Her academic areas of achievement were creative writing and philosophy. She said that although she could not spell, her ability to think creatively led to success in both subjects. She is also artistic.

☆☆ Human Capital ☆☆
Talent Management:
How to Strategize,
Attract, Evaluate,
Develop, and Lead

6

☆ ☆ The Human ☆ ☆ Resources Division

Finally, a Chance to Shine

If you're asking for a seat at the table, I think you've missed the point.
—Susan Meisinger, President and CEO of the
Society for Human Resource Management

The Personnel Department Evolves into the Human Resources Division: What Next?

Let's first determine exactly what changed when the personnel department became the human resources (HR) division. Some say nothing; however, I don't believe that to be the case. Understanding the historic evolution of the personnel department's function allows you to predict the future and therefore leap ahead of competitors when it comes to optimizing human capital management.

The personnel department, in its early years, was basically an administrative record-keeping function. It was about knowing who the employees were and getting them registered on the payroll; in some cases, getting them health and retirement benefits and maintaining the infamous employee personnel file.

Now fast-forward a few decades and personnel begins to offer training and contribute to the actual running of the business. Albeit it is a baby step, but a step forward just the same. That modest transformation was the first indication of the future of HR. Moving from stodgy, mundane record keeper to trainer began personnel's growth trajectory toward HR. From that point, let's review some history and make some forward-looking predictions—here is what has already happened and what will happen:

The Transformation

Stage One

- The focus of the personnel function shifted from record keeping to making tactical business contributions.
- The contributions came in the form of training—both cultural training so that new employees understood the ways of the organization and technical training so that employees could operate machines, manage staff, fill-out employee evaluations, and the like.

Stage Two

- Personnel expanded from providing training to offering organizational development services, such as asking: How should we organize? Who should report to whom? How should employees be evaluated? What sort of pay-grade system should be adopted?

All this happened with *risk avoidance* as the driving mentality of the personnel function and therefore of the personnel department. In our simplified history, HR's evolution spans about a 50-year period (Stages 1 and 2). To say the evolution was slow is an understatement. Personnel was a highly tactical rather than a strategic function. However, who was to blame for the slow evolution and was this really a problem? The answers are that *both* the organization's leadership and its personnel professionals were to blame, and perhaps the slow evolution was not a problem until recently. Let's continue with the history:

Stage Three

- Personnel takes on responsibility for the **tactical** adminis-tration of employee records, compensation and benefits, training, employee relations, organizational development, and employment (e.g., staffing, recruiting, labor relations) with many resultant subsets in each of these broad categories. Personnel has moved from a clerical function to a profession. There are now generalists and specialists. Personnel departments are becoming pretty big and administratively important to the workings of the organization. We just covered another 10 years of evolution, but personnel has not yet become strategic. Why? Read on!

Stage Four

- Now, personnel is a profession, so it needed to change its label. Hence, *Human Resources* was born.

- Human Resources does not yet have a seat at the table, but it gets invited into the room—sometimes to take notes, and sometimes to make presentations.

- A turbulent period begins where HR has a chance to break through and win a seat at the table, but it is not being given to HR easily. So, some organizations (a select few) have HR leaders truly taking risks and helping to drive the business, while other organizations are stuck in the personnel legacy—big time inertia.

INERTIA: THE ULTIMATE IMPEDIMENT TO PROGRESS

I think The Bank of New York is a great institution. I learned valuable lessons while working there and made many friends as well so I am not being critical of the Bank in this example. It is actually a great firsthand illustration of the evolution of HR. When I joined The Bank of New York in 1987, the company had a personnel department. It consisted of several personnel groups such as Operations Personnel and others, but the function was not called HR. There were thousands of employees, and hundreds of bank locations, but no HR division; personnel would do just fine. The Bank was founded by Alexander Hamilton and certainly has a rich history, but with history comes inertia. The need to transform from a personnel culture of paper-pushing "administrivia" to an HR culture of tactical and eventual strategic contribution was a distant concept in the industry. The Bank eventually got there in name; the HR division was born. Like many organizations, however, the name changed more dramatically than the actual function. The interesting but logical thing about all this is that the slow evolution happened everywhere, and it was okay. The gradual change happened because the business leaders in organizations were not conditioned to have a strategic human capital partner at their sides. They knew personnel: If you needed a form, wanted to advertise for a job, or needed details on the company picnic, personnel was there. Hence, personnel was pigeon-holed by its history—inertia.

Thank God for Adam Smith. He didn't invent business process transformation, but he defined how it happens without consultants, study groups, and white papers. He explained that change happens by necessity; it is inevitable when not obstructed by outside forces, and so we can now predict the future of the HR evolution. The *moment of inertia* has been broken. Modern HR dynamics are finally taking hold.

Stage Five

- The HR division will become the most critical operating group in the organization; it will be the heartbeat of the business. The chief HR officer will emerge alongside the chief information officer (CIO), the chief financial officer (CFO), and others.

- The HR organization will not be a record keeper; it will be an outsourcer of record keeping. As it did 25 years ago for the payroll function, it does and will continue to do for most other administrative tasks.

- The HR division will be the mission critical provider of talent, developer of talent, deployer of talent, predictor of talent needs, and keeper of the corporate culture(s). With globalization, there will not be a single corporate culture as we know it; there will be several cultures that make up the organization, and yes, that means there will be organizational diversity too.

When I mention that HR is to be the predictor of talent needs and the deployer of talent, I begin to shed light on HR as a strategic, not just tactical contributor. Yes, it really is happening and, not a moment too soon.

Since 1974, Lee Hecht Harrison, a sister company to our firm, has proudly gained a reputation for understanding the changing world of work and is a leader in talent management and leadership development.

The folks at Lee Hecht Harrison say their clients frequently tell them:

- I need help recruiting, developing, and retaining high-potential employees.
- I need help designing and implementing a process to ensure our realigned executive team will lead effectively to meet specific business goals.
- We have a new performance management process and our employees need help creating meaningful development plans.
- I need help designing a leadership program that will support our current business initiatives.
- We need to help our managers understand their role in reducing key employee turnover.

- We have had tremendous change in our organization and our employees are asking for ways to take charge of their careers.

- We need to help our managers have effective development conversations with their employees.

- We need help identifying and developing leadership behaviors in our succession candidates.

- I would like to help a newly hired executive quickly adapt to our culture and have an immediate impact on our business.

- I would like a process that is more effective than just a training program to develop leadership skills in middle-level managers.

I especially like the statement about the client seeking a more effective *process* rather than just a training program—remember when the conduct of the training was the deliverable: *We held the class so now we can check the box.* Businesses are now seeking a process that is more than training classes and is a sequential flow of integrated activities that will result in learning. That sounds like an actual corporate culture shift with talent management embodied at the core of its being. Finally, and NOT A MOMENT TOO SOON.

If HR is to address the needs of business, it needs the same budgetary attention that we give to the information technology (IT) organization. The HR department is not a budget area to cut anymore. If companies invest in this area, they will reap great rewards, assuming the HR leader spends wisely. There is no shortage of things to buy. The sale of tools and services to HR leaders is a multibillion-dollar industry.

Human Resources Is a Sophisticated Service Provider

The HR organization is a services company within the company. At least, that is the attitude that I encourage HR leaders to have. They need to make the business case for HR as a business unit with a real return on investment; and that means getting the right plan and organizational design to win the budget needed to get the job done. Run HR like you would run a business; have an outsourcer's mentality.

The Head of Human Resources as Chief Executive Officer

The HR division has a clear mission and a very complicated job. That is why HR leaders at all levels need to adopt a real business approach to what they do. They need to wake up every morning believing that they are running a business and that they are the CEOs of their units. The "staff mentality" in HR has got to go. All this is easier said than done. Most HR leaders have been brought up over the past 20 years to be involved in the business on the periphery, without a seat at the table; they have been satisfied in a staff role. This sort of mentality cannot prevail in the Talent Age. Human Resources is finally front and center—every business situation will challenge HR to have the talent solution. Entire strategies will hinge on HR the way they have hinged on IT for the past two decades. This era can be HR's finest hour.

The HR organization needs to identify talent needs and craft a set of solutions. It is just that clear—not simple, but very clear. With this in mind, just as in the past, the division will choose to handle some aspects of the job internally, and they will buy services for other needs.

DOING IT RIGHT, RIGHT NOW

But before they buy products and services, HR and businesses need to have a battle plan. Progressive, enlightened leaders in HR and business units are seeing the future, and more important, they're not afraid to let go of the past. However, some business leaders today are a bit like shipwreck victims. The boat they're in is going down, but they're nervous about jumping into the lifeboats. Eventually, some of those who get in the lifeboats and row hard are going to find a bigger, better ship to pick them up. Some are going to sink. The ones left on the first ship are going down regardless. However, the enlightened ones are finding ways to right the ship and make new headway.

Figure 6.1 demonstrates what's keeping current CEOs and smart HR leaders awake at night.

Deloitte concludes that:

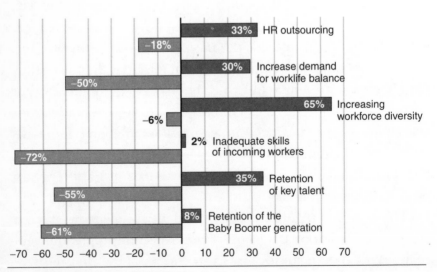

Figure 6.1 Workforce issues affecting business performance.

Powerful forces are shaping today's workforce and hampering companies' ability to attract and retain the talent they need to meet business priorities. An aging executive population is marked by widespread Baby Boomer retirements. More than 40 percent of managers in traditional companies are soon eligible for retirement. Replacing them is a daunting task, as consolidation and reorganization have eliminated many positions that formerly served as training grounds for future leaders.[1]

This is what we've been discussing for the past few chapters. This is the fire-bell being rung in the night. Who's going to wake up and be saved? Who's going to sleep through it and perish? You not only have to replace these lost Baby Boomers, you have to replace them with the right new workers. In a sense, the United States has a golden opportunity right when it needs one. The Baby Boomers are going out with a bang (or maybe a whimper, we'll see), but that opens up so much fresh opportunity and territory to be replanted the right way, through the newest techniques. Frankly, if many of these people weren't going to retire soon, you might have to ax them.

Think of it like the great Chicago fire. Mrs. O'Leary's famous cow knocked over an oil lamp and half the city burned to the ground overnight. That was a total disaster, right? Wrong, aside from the terrible loss of life, it was a great opportunity— one of the greatest in history. They got to rebuild an *entire city* with an eye on the future. As long as they did it right, it was a great good. The people in Chicago did it right and the city went on to become the second most prosperous city in the United States in the twentieth century. In a human capital sense, the United States is again getting an equal, and probably greater, opportunity with the retirement of the Baby Boomers.

How to Drive More Value through Talent Management Strategies

People don't leave companies, they leave managers. That statement is largely true. Talent management strategy is relatively simple to diagram, but to execute it is indeed complicated. Traditional talent management strategies around employee retention focused on rich compensation packages and special bonuses—all of which could be matched by competitors—instead of what people really want from a career. People want to look forward to going to work in the morning. That's pretty basic. That doesn't mean they don't want a challenge, it means they want to feel empowered, resourced, and positioned to compete effectively. It's challenge and intrinsic fulfillment that keeps most employees happy. Hertzberg's theories taught us in Psychology 101 that wages are a "hygiene" factor—they won't motivate us, they'll simply keep us from becoming unmotivated. We all know this, yet we rarely implement much more than compensation plans and award programs to try and address the issue. We need to build a culture that creates a stimulating, positive environment. In small companies, the employee retention profile is usually at one extreme or the other—people tend to stay or the place is fraught with constant turnover. This reminds me of a story that one of our key employees, Dan Gonzalez, repeats when he talks about Cornell International in our early years. It seems that a large search firm tried to recruit him away from us. We were a small company. They asked him how much it would take to attract him to join them. He said, "You couldn't pay me enough." They said, "Yes, we can, just let us know what the number needs to be." He said, "That's my point, you couldn't *pay* me enough." The fact is they could have paid him much more money, but he stayed because of the culture. We were on a mission—a journey—and employees gladly reject money when they like where they work and where they're going.

If you've been following along, this should ring a few bells. Who are these "committed" workers you're going to start hiring? South Polers—people who are passionate about what they do. It's up to you to give them work to be passionate about, but given that, they're the ones who are going to drive your company through the obstacle course of the new millennium. So you've cleared away the dead wood and have to start reseeding your north 40 with the best new talent. Now what?

This could be the topic of yet another book, but Chapter 7 will have to suffice. There are variations of this model in the marketplace, but I feel this articulation is the most powerful. If HR is to shine, it has to execute the following talent management model effectively:

1. *Strategize:* This suggests that you adopt your business strategy and forecast your talent needs.

2. *Attract:* Go get the additional talent needed for this strategy from within or outside your organization. Some position this as the point where you *acquire* talent, but I think the answer to talent acquisition is indeed talent attraction. You need to think beyond fetching talent to the point where your company sees that its responsibility is to constantly *attract* talent. In simple terms, this is the recruiting phase.

3. *Deploy:* My favorite plan is, "attack-attack-attack." Assign the talent to the field with clear deliverables and measurable outcomes.

4. *Evaluate:* Look at the measurable outcomes and see how the performance ranks. Utilize self-assessment, 360 feedback, and other methods of measurement.

Measure performance against metrics, requirements, desired outcomes, and deliverables.

5. *Develop:* Based on the needed skills and past performance measurements, adopt an appropriate talent development program with skills training, knowledge exchange, mentoring, and a host of other techniques.

6. *Retain:* Create an appealing culture through rewards, *esprit d' corps,* opportunity, and collegiality and camaraderie.

7. *Re-strategize:* Continue proactive thinking. Remember, the environment is dynamic—things have already changed.

Is all this talent management stuff brand-new? Haven't hard-working, imaginative, passionate North and South Poler employees always contributed to companies and other enterprises throughout history? Yes, but the difference is that talent management must now receive the same sort of serious attention that we gave to technology management in the final part of the twentieth century. Remember the Carnegie Mellon technology model that put forth a standard for dealing with technology management and applications development? We have paid a lot of attention to software application development, endeavoring to put forth a replicable model for success. Our human capital talent management model now needs the same sort of attention.

Capitalizing on Human Capital Management

One good thing about the faster, more-connected Information Age is that along with the increased competition comes far more readily available tools than ever before. Most of them are even free. Take, for example, the Human Capital In-

stitute (HCI). They have free online seminars and other resources that are, like gold in the streets, just laying there waiting to be gathered up by the opportunist. The Human Capital
Institute is a not-for-profit membership organization, a think
tank, and an educational resource for professionals and business executives. They are at the forefront of this new talent
management movement. The chairman of Human Capital Institute, Michael Foster, has this to say about the current state
of affairs:

> Strategic talent management is the most important competitive
> lever in the global knowledge economy, yet most organizations
> are still operating with industrial-era practices in HR and line
> management. We are at an inflection point where intangible as-
> sets, including human and intellectual capital, have become the
> primary drivers of market value. In a marketplace of rapid and
> continuous change, organizations that excel at attracting, en-
> gaging and leading top talent will increasingly pull ahead.
> HCI's mission is to help companies understand and embrace
> this human capital paradigm shift, and drive a talent mind-set
> through the enterprise with research, education and action.[2]

The Human Capital Institute sounds like the kind of club
every CEO should join. All good things in the Talent Age are
going to stem from identifying, attracting, evaluating, developing, and retaining new employees, managers, and the top-
tier executives from both poles.

The landscape in front of us shows a quickly fragmenting
HR arena. Some activities remain internal while a host of others are outsourced. In some ways, we are moving from the
structure of the HR generalist overseeing the vertical functions of employment, compensation and benefits, and training
and development to a more spherical model, with talent management at the core, with those vertical functions wrapped

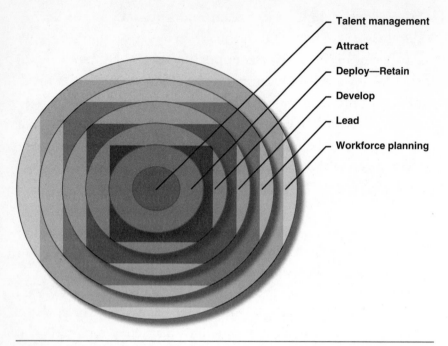

Figure 6.2   Spherical Human Resources model (Guarino, 2006).

around the core to create the layers needed for a total solution
(see Figure 6.2).

THE TALENT AGE STILL NEEDS TECHNOLOGY

We can't address this topic without paying some attention to
the technology solutions that can be brought to bear. There
are now a host of strategic technologies available to assist in
this endeavor. The solutions range from enterprise wide applications to best-in-class niche applications apart from a more
overarching enterprise solutions provider. The option of business process outsourcing (BPO) is now very viable as well.
Some aspects of the HR function are no longer mission critical
and can easily be outsourced for greater efficiency and re-
duced labor cost. Just as ADP and PayChex showed us that pay-

roll outsourcing made sense, a host of other activities will soon be rationalized for BPO.

Multinationals are not immune to this sea change. Because such businesses manage talent across global markets, a complex array of issues must be confronted. Beyond basic language barriers, talent management must confront issues such as how to standardize retention and recruitment efforts with different cultural drivers. They must also deal with currency arbitrage as massive payrolls float in volatile foreign exchange environments. They must address risk management as it relates to employee's physical security in an increasingly dangerous geopolitical environment. Data protection laws create regulatory risks, and staff must be fully aware of local legislation not only across the country but also across the world.

Now that we are truly running businesses where our human capital talent is a mission critical resource, we need to find ways to measure the real contribution that talent is making to our overall financial success. If HR leaders are going to justify the talent management function being well funded, they are going to have to show a measurable return on investment. How does the investment improve profitability? It is not as easy as a cost-benefit analysis used to justify capital expenditures to improve manufacturing equipment on an assembly line. Indeed, our companies are running increasingly more on "human machinery" that produces in accordance with its level of talent. However, we do not have the metrics or the measurement tools in place to provide the basis for adequate analysis. The CIO will need to see the HR division as a critical customer. The HR systems will need decision algorithms to screen and refine data and information. And this is just the beginning.

There is a massive list of questions that must be addressed as HR transforms. It really is a whole new world out there. Like NASA in the 1960s, you're going to need a cadre of specially trained and superbly conditioned people to go out and conquer it. New technology tends to get the headlines because it's so colorful. But you still need someone to not only properly employ the latest technologies but also intelligently assess which technologies are worth investing in. It still all boils down to people; the right people.

7

☆ ☆ Strategize to ☆ ☆ Optimize Talent

Talent Road Mapping and the Talent Inventory

If you don't know where you're going, there's a good chance you'll end up someplace else and *certainly with the* wrong *people.*

—Alan Guarino

Workforce planning has been a reactive process at best. Companies have taken business initiatives and then, almost as an afterthought, began to consider the talent ramifications. Today, companies are finally taking workforce planning to a new height. Imagine having the ability to create a workforce model that enables you to invest in talent in direct proportion to the talent's actual contribution to the organization. Now imagine that you can apply this model to the smallest operating groups in the organization, taking into account both geography and the actual job functions.

You need to do more than just imagine this happening; you need to *do* this to remain competitive. I call the process *Talent Road Mapping*. In managing a global workforce or just a regional operation, you must be able to:

- Manage head count and talent-related investments by location and job function
- Measure talent supply as well as overages and shortages that are attrition related, performance related, and *always* in respect to the business objectives.

The Talent Road Mapping process leads to a *Talent Inventory* that allows you to see the disposition of your talent resources from the perspective of job function, geography, and business alignment.

To optimize the talent in any organization, the leadership needs to follow this talent road map. From my days as an army officer, I recall that planning always included potential risks along the route to our objective. So when putting together a talent plan, you not only need to map out the talent needed to achieve success but also anticipate the pitfalls and attempt to mitigate problems in advance. When this is purely a soft people-driven process, the risks include:

- Intrinsic and extrinsic bias that clouds the objective review of the talent on your team. (Visit http://www.armc-hr.com to learn more.)

- People may try to match the objective to the talent at hand rather than matching the talent to the objective. Beware the pitfall of "We'll go where our talent can take us" rather than going where the strategy deems necessary.

- The constantly shifting sand of the marketplace requires an ability to predict the future but create an *agile* plan that can shift as the future unfolds.

The Talent Road Mapping process assumes that you know where the organization is going and consists of the following:

- *Talent assessment:* What capabilities do I have and what do I need?

- *Talent shortfall:* Which specific capabilities are currently understaffed?

- *Talent overage:* Which specific capabilities are in greater abundance than needed?

This process leads you to your current *Talent Inventory.* Once you know your shortfalls and your overages, you can begin to specify the action steps along the route to your objective. Specifically, the action steps address:

- The overage situation needs to be rectified by reassigning employees elsewhere within the organization (to someone else's shortfall area) or through downsizing.
- The shortfalls must then be solved through reallocation from within the organization where someone else's overage provides the talent that fits your area of shortfall. The additional shortfall needs to be solved through outside talent acquisition—recruiting.

RECRUITING FOR MANAGEMENT TALENT IS LIKE MAKING AN ACQUISITION

The Talent Inventory approach should become a cornerstone within your talent management culture. Business leaders and their human resources (HR) colleagues should eat, breathe, and sleep this aspect of your business. This is a process that never ends. At a minimum, a Talent Inventory should be conducted each time a new initiative is launched to make sure that tunnel vision has not led you to deploy with the wrong set of capabilities; namely, deploying people already on staff rather than the best people for the job. Ask yourself if you would have actually *hired* the individuals you have in the assigned roles had they come from outside the company.

Some companies take the Talent Inventory to new heights. Although commercial software solutions for workforce planning are in scarce supply, they do have the potential to serve HR departments well by automating the process and even mitigating some of the risks. One company that offers a cutting edge software solution in line with my concept of Talent Road Mapping is Vemo, headed by Peter Louch. The software allows

you to identify your talent needs and plan for resource alloca-
tion to optimize your talent solution. Using custom software solutions is an ideal way to effectively execute on the complex,
tedious process of workforce planning.

According to Peter, senior executives are starting to view
workforce planning as the area of talent management that has
the greatest potential impact on the business. Paul Dumas, executive vice president of HR at Agere Systems and a client of
Vemo, explains:

> The level of effort organizations put behind their workforce
> planning is the number one differentiator between mediocre
> and highly effective and high-performing organizations. There
> is no sense in investing in talent if you don't intend to maximize
> that investment.[1]

Peter Louch believes that if you are a chief executive in a
typical organization, and your organization spends 30 percent
to 40 percent of its annual revenue on people and programs,
you would want to know how well this massive investment is
working for your organization. But when you start to look for a
workforce plan, you might find it incomplete or, worse yet,
missing altogether. If you are typical, you will probably not
find any experienced workforce planners in your organization.
How could this be?

Perhaps, it is because workforce planning has so many moving parts. It requires the workforce planner to partner with
line executives to understand business strategies and what
roles are critical to those strategies. Workforce planning requires a planner who is adept at change management, able to
sell the plan internally, and to perform skilled financial analysis. This planner must be an expert in HR, knowing all the ter-
minology, where to look, and what the talent management
implications will be. Until recently, there have not been any

tools commercially available to harness all of the moving parts, turn the requirements into a job description, and try to find the candidate who can meet all of these requirements and who is willing to build her or his own tool.

It is not a huge surprise that very few organizations have historically conducted proactive workforce planning. With this in mind, it's clear that software solutions are an excellent tool for workforce planners who want to hit the ground running.

At Vemo, Peter Louch saw a huge opportunity that could be solved through a new type of software tool that provides a comprehensive workforce planning process and corresponding tool set. The process would help workforce planners actually transform information about the business into a clear and shared understanding of what talent is critical, enabling workforce planners to develop a talent investment model that combines the *strategic perspective* of executives, the *budgetary perspective* of finance, the *demand for talent* by line executives, and the understanding of the *supply* of internal and external talent. This tool embeds the difficult math and financial analysis in the process so that the workforce planner can stay out of the weeds and stay focused on the big picture. Vemo's process aggregates all of the human resource details into the data views necessary to make quality planning decisions and answers the following questions:

- For our most critical talent, are we better than our competitors?
- What are our projected gaps, not only in numbers, but also in capability and performance?
- For which talent populations can we carefully manage attrition so we can better afford the investments in critical

talent that will drive our business? What is work we should no longer be doing at all?

A software-enabled process allows workforce planners, and HR in general, to focus on dialogue with the line executives to understand business needs and help line executives project what talent will drive competitive advantage instead of looking at past successes. The planning becomes a natural extension of the dialogue, instead of a brick wall. With a better understanding of the size and priorities of talent gaps, talent management can become a proactive function that has enough lead time to recruit, redeploy, develop, engage, and retain the talent that matters most to the business. Peter solicited input about this from Kevin Pennington, chief HR officer of Rogers Communication, who says:

> Without planning you may have a collection of good talent management programs and thinking, but everyone is talking past each other, and there is no consistent progress on improving the business. Planning brings the current and future business needs into focus and ensures that HR is making a meaningful impact on business results.[2]

Having considered critical tools in the Talent Road Mapping process, now let's look at how one company has actually mobilized around workforce planning at the senior most level. The Thomson Corporation, led by Richard Harrington, is a great example of managing a critical talent pool of its top 500 management professionals, I heard that Bill Gates once said if you took 20 key people out of Microsoft, the company would be finished. Thomson's not taking any such chances. The Thomson Corporation has an established global approach in place. Kathleen McCarthy, who leads Thomson's talent acquisition efforts, and Mark Kizilos, who leads the talent management function, explained Thomson's strategy to me in the following way.

Developing Talent Is Becoming an Imperative

The Thomson Corporation has transformed itself through acquisitions. Thomson has evolved from a holding company where success was dependent on the effective management of financial assets to an operating company where the business proposition is dependent on the ability to offer solutions that integrate and leverage the diverse set of assets. This shift has made the identification and development of enterprisewide leaders—those with deep experience in Thomson's markets and the breadth to lead complex organizations—an essential focus for the recruiting and talent management teams. A primary means of developing that capability is by moving key talent across the organization to expand their perspective and build leadership skills.

Moving Talent to Develop Broader Leadership Capability

It is important to bring new talent into the organization at senior levels, but there are distinct advantages to creating a robust talent growth engine within the organization. Internal movement of high-talent individuals to provide stretch assignments is a powerful experience-based component of the development approach at Thomson. Moving talent across the organization develops individuals by exposing them to a broader perspective and expanding their skill sets through experience. At the same time, it contributes to a stronger bench of leaders to drive the growth of the business.

Ongoing studies of employee engagement at Thomson reinforce the philosophy by demonstrating that the most talented employees are motivated by job and career development opportunities. When they see that outstanding performance is rewarded with career opportunities and advancement, these valued employees become more engaged in their present job, and are more likely to stay and flourish as high performing leaders for Thomson. As an additional benefit, the talent development and career opportunities created by the focus on internal recruiting contribute to the organization's reputation as a desirable place to work.

Driving Talent Movement through Key Operating Mechanisms

Every year, the business and corporate leaders of Thomson meet to refine their growth strategy and align their talent management efforts to support it. The strategy and talent management processes comprise two of the primary operating mechanisms that Thomson's CEO, Richard Harrington, uses to set the tone and direction that guide the organization. Each spring, the organization's leaders meet in person to fine-tune the growth strategy for each Thomson business. Then in the summer, they meet again to discuss the skills needed to execute that strategy. They review hundreds of managers and identify development opportunities for each. The CEO personally invests several weeks of his time in this process, discussing the top 500 to 600 managers in the company. Strategy development and talent management are very closely linked. The talent meetings ensure that Thomson has the right people with the right skills in the right positions to implement its strategy successfully.

Leveraging the Talent Inventory

Shortly after the organization's strategic-planning process is complete, members of Thomson's executive committee assess current and emerging leaders across the organization through the talent review process. In the talent review sessions, which take place during the summer, rich dialogue with each division's leadership team brings focus on strengths, development needs, and development plans for key individuals. Executives are profiled using an in-house talent management system that creates a concise, one-page profile with information about prior work experience, significant performance hits and misses, leadership strengths, mobility, career aspirations, and assessments using the Thomson Leadership Competencies. In addition, a one-page development plan is included to guide the individual's development. This plan is discussed during the talent review process and can be the catalyst for the movement of key career objectives and the needs of the business.

While individuals move across the organization, typically only a few enterprisewide moves stem directly from specific conversations in the review session. The broader purpose of the sessions is to inventory the organization's talent. The Talent Inventory and the insight gained are then leveraged in various decisions made throughout the year relating to recruiting and executive learning and development programs.

The Thomson recruiting organization has been designed to benefit from its internal executive candidate pool. Specifically, each division has a dedicated senior recruiter who is focused on executive recruiting and facilitates all internal talent movement. Through Thomson's talent management team, recruitment is able to leverage the Talent Inventory and source internal talent for key openings in a manner that meets business needs and develops talent.

Sourcing Internal Talent

Consistent with the recruiting philosophy, which emphasizes internal movement, the first step in filling any executive opening is to create an internal candidate slate. The slate is developed by searching information that was vetted in the talent review sessions. Internal candidates are identified and screened using various criteria such as their leadership potential, ratings on the Thomson Leadership Competencies, skills, experience, mobility, and career readiness. In addition, slates being created for critical or highly developmental positions are flagged to ensure that high-potential individuals who are ready for a new position receive consideration.

High Quality Internal Candidate Slates

Once the preliminary slate is developed, Thomson's recruiters follow up to further vet the list, determine whether the candidate can be moved from their current position, and assess potential interest. In cases where high-potential candidates are not available to move due to business priorities, the individual is informed that the organization considered them for the opportunity. This discussion is focused on communicating to the individual that they are valued and will have ongoing career opportunities.

Ongoing Functional Talent Movement Discussions

In addition to the candidate slate process, various Thomson functions hold bimonthly discussions to review talent movement. In these discussions, the leaders of the functions from across the organization review both current and anticipated open positions. These discussions result in explicit strategic movement of top talent across the organization.

Senior Executive Visibility into Talent Movement

The commitment to sourcing talent internally is reinforced through a monthly senior executive review of all open executive positions globally.

A Dramatic Turnaround

The focus on talent movement at Thomson has contributed to a marked improvement in their ability to manage leadership succession by filling key positions with qualified internal talent. In 1997, Thomson filled approximately 25 percent of its leadership positions with internally developed talent. Since then, this figure has risen to over 75 percent of leadership openings are filled annually with internal talent. While the recruiting and talent management practices have played a major role in achieving the results, a significant contributing factor is Thomson's progress in evolving a learning culture through the joint efforts of the HR team and business leadership.

Thomson's commitment to continuous talent growth allows for a flexible and agile organization with the ability to shift seamlessly as the business evolves.

Workforce planning will lead to a dynamic staffing plan so that you can set out to find the talent you need, employing a South Pole strategy as a big part of your talent acquisition component. Our overall talent pool is in dangerously short supply. Leave no stone unturned.

8

☆ ☆ **Attract South Polers** ☆ ☆
and Other Talent

Find the Needle in the Haystack

The 2001 Maritz Poll contends that as many as 49 percent of employees were compelled to apply for their positions because of the strength of their employers' brand—the company's image *as an employer.*

—*Safari Solutions Newsletter,* April 2006

thers use the term *talent acquisition* and it is a good label. I also like to use the phrase *talent attraction* to emphasize the competitive nature of recruiting. The paradigm has shifted from employees in search of a job, to employers in search of talent. The talent holds all the cards. It is a sellers market and will remain so for at least the foreseeable future. While every hire is indeed a mini-acquisition and should be treated with serious diligence, you won't even get the chance to make that hire if you don't have an employer brand to *attract* talent.

What impressions do candidates have of your company as an employer? Are they vague or misleading? If so, it's time to create an *employer brand.* Read on for suggestions.

STAND OUT FROM THE CROWD—MARKETING FOR TALENT 101

From a product-marketing perspective, we all certainly appreciate the value of branding. It conveys a powerful message before the customer even gets into the specifics of the product. It makes people want to buy. Examples of branding are Rolls Royce and Rolex to name a few. If we see the talent pool as a group of customers, the ones we would like to sell on a career with our company, we can better understand the value of branding as an employer. You might understand this, but I bet you're not doing it. I recently had this conversation with a CEO. He completely understood the employer branding proposition, so I tested him and asked:

- How much is your marketing department spending to raise your brand as an employer, or are they just working on your product marketing?
- Who is your vice president of employer branding?
- How much have you allocated in your human resources (HR) budget specifically for employer branding?

You may have thought about employer branding, but have you truly acted on it? Okay, so I won that round. Remember the Honda commercial about the car that sells itself—a strong employer brand makes talent acquisition much easier. It becomes *talent attraction.*

As with any product or service, branding has to reflect reality or the customer will quickly discover the sham. Branding only conveys reality if you are truly an "employer of choice." That is what you need to be to attract and ultimately retain all this talent.

When trying to create a model to support employer-of-choice branding, look to the traits found in small entrepreneurial companies. Why? Because they are not large and multifaceted, they have some of the key elements of a strong employer-of-choice program. When people work for these companies, they are very committed to the company's mission. Small companies have an intimacy that large companies have difficulty creating. These small organizations are familial—they work and play hard. Employees are free to disagree openly with one another about business decisions, yet hold little animosity or political baggage. Basically, people work there because it feels right, not for the wages they are paid—often, larger companies would pay them more—but they know the mission and enjoy the journey. Once the company gets large and successful, these people often leave the organization saying that they no longer feel part of the organization they *loved*. That's right, loved. A great company has employees who *love* where they work. How do small companies do it? This is what you are shooting for:

- Leaders are visible—not hidden from view and interaction—in an office.
- Everyone is focused on expenses and sales (cash flow is king).
- New ideas are accepted and expected because there is no "that's how we've always done it" mentality.
- People take personal responsibility and are genuinely recognized for their contributions.
- Employees receive hands-on training; often from their direct supervisor or even the CEO.
- The company celebrates its successes.
- There is a feeling of team spirit that is created by physically working together in a single location.
- The mission is clear and direct so that everyone:
    —Knows who the customer is.
    —Knows what is expected of them in their roles.
    —Knows where and to whom to go for help.
    —Feels appreciated.
    —Feels proud of the company (often with a swagger).

Christine Johnson at Shaker, the employment advertising company, wrote an article on employee branding in which she described what an employer brand does. She put it this way:

> It conveys your "value proposition"—the totality of your culture, systems, attitudes, and employee relationship. And it encourages your people to embrace and further shared

goals—success, productivity, and satisfaction—on personal and professional levels.[1]

When it comes to a strong employer brand, the value proposition Christine Johnson mentioned embodies all the small company traits listed earlier. The company must be one where people love to work. They do so because they are listened to, empowered to act, motivated by visible leaders, aware of the company's mission and direction, and rewarded for their contributions and sacrifices. A healthy company is required for a genuinely healthy employer brand. If you have built such an environment, you still need the marketing communications, both internally and externally, to promote what you have created. To achieve this, you need someone who is responsible for the employer branding mission.

Watson Wyatt, the noted HR consulting company, found that superior human capital practices create significant shareholder value; employer branding is a valued part of the practices that create value.

Companies with superior human capital practices can create more than double the shareholder value than companies with average human capital practices, according to Watson Wyatt's Human Capital Index® (HCI) studies in Europe, Asia-Pacific, and North America. The findings provide the first-ever documentation that the strong link between human capital practices and shareholder value creation stretches across several continents.

The HCI studies of companies in Europe, Asia-Pacific, and North America report on the impact of human capital practices on business performance. Their combined database includes more than 2,000 major companies globally and tracks shareholder performance from 1994 to 2002.

"While each regional study carries some cultural differences, the results demonstrate that great HR practices can be a true competitive advantage," said J. P. Orbeta, global director of Watson Wyatt's Human Capital practice. "Now we have seen that superior human capital practices prevail, regardless of economic conditions or geographic location."*

Watson Wyatt's Human Capital Index Global Truths

The studies report that companies have better total returns to shareholders (TRS) or growth in shareholder value if they have the following superior human capital practices:

★ *Clear rewards and accountability:* A 16.5 percent to 21.5 percent increase is associated with practices such as broad-based stock ownership, paying above the market, and effective performance management.

★ *Excellence in recruitment and retention:* A 5.4 percent to 14.6 percent increase is associated with practices such as an effective recruiting process, a positive employer brand, and focus on key skills retention.

★ *Collegial, flexible workplaces:* A 9.0 percent to 21.5 percent increase is associated with practices such as employee input into how the work gets done, higher trust in senior management, and a lack of workplace hierarchy.

★ *Communications integrity:* A 2.6 percent to 7.1 percent increase is associated with practices such as effective use of employee surveys, sharing of strategy and financial data with employees, and employee input into decision making.

---

* www.watsonwyatt.com (January 30, 2003).

Once your company assigns responsibility for employer branding, the chosen individuals should consider the following model:

Employer Branding 101

Key Components Needed to Successfully Brand

- *Corporate identity:* This is what and who you are as the employer, including your values, environment, temperament, and vision. These are the inward-looking traits that describe your organization.

- *Corporate differentiator:* What makes you a compelling employer versus other choices in the marketplace? This is the set of facts that allow you to clearly illustrate differences between working for you and working for one of your competitors. Just as you would do when differentiating your product positioning in a classic product marketing scenario.

- *Communications:* These are the methods and messages needed to convey your value proposition. Just as in product marketing, these communications will be tailored to the specific employee community you are addressing— executive, technology, finance, sales, exempt, nonexempt, and so on.

The Branding Methodology

- *Identify:* What is the scope of the effort? How will you implement it—through regional units, vertical by centers of excellence, globally, or by operating units?

- *State:* What are the desired outcomes and how they will be measured?

- *Assess:* What are the "before" employee perceptions? Conduct employee interviews and surveys to learn how much the company is or is not "loved" by employees.

- *Sort:* Organize the surveyed employee perceptions as "valid" or "invalid." Fix the problems that are valid (easier said than done, but you have to be healthy before you can have a healthy brand). Use extra emphasis in your message to rectify the misperceptions where employee beliefs are not valid—there is a misunderstanding.

You are now ready to attract talent, but you're still not ready to recruit. To discuss talent attraction, talent acquisition, recruiting, or whatever you want to call it, you must first understand the landscape. This is the most dangerous time ever in the history of recruitment. The stakes have never been higher, the market has never been messier, and the competition is getting fiercer every day. There are now four major solutions available to handle recruitment, as well as blending or mixing and matching them. For ease of discussion, let's look at them as free-standing operations:

1. *Retained executive search:* With this service, clients receive high-touch, highly consultative recruiting support aimed at filling jobs that pay $100,000 or more in cash compensation. The search firm is paid its fee regardless of whether they actually fill the position. Typically, it is best used for positions that pay $300,000 or more in cash compensation.

2. *Contingency recruiting:* This service fills jobs on an "as can" basis and is only paid a fee if they fill the job with one of their candidates. This is best used for positions that are somewhat commoditized or when the mission criticality of the position is not enough to justify a higher-priced retained search service.

3. *Contingent staffing:* We used to call this *temporary employment* when it began in force in the 1970s. Contingent staffing now ranges from filling positions in

call centers, mail rooms, and warehouses to interim executive placements and a broad range of specialty services. The industry is separated into three major sections:

- *General staffing:* Nonexempt positions paying $50,000 or less.
- *Professional staffing:* Hourly paid "consultants" in accounting, finance, engineering, and technology. Cost ranges from $30 per hour to $800 or more per day, per employee.
- *Interim executive staffing:* Paid by the day at a long-term or short-term assignment rate, this is for management positions ranging from CEO to senior departmental leaders who are brought in to fill a void while a company is in turnaround mode or while an executive search is being conducted to fill the role with a permanent employee. These positions cost $1,500 to more than $2,500 per day to fill.

These solutions are all outside services that an organization can use to fill positions. In-house recruiting is as another solution:

4. *Internal talent acquisition:* While organizations have always sought to fill roles without using external support (they did so by running ads and using employee referrals), the approach was usually a far cry from what the outside recruiting organizations provided. However, the internal recruiting solution is now becoming highly sophisticated. Organizations are building the equivalent of the outside recruiting organizations as internal units. Fidelity Investments has the equivalent of a contingent staffing company, and companies like Time Warner and Google have

what some would say approaches the service level of an outside retained search organization.

One Way to Attract Talent—The Internal Solution

Time Warner's approach works something like this. When Cormac Culihane left Korn Ferry and took on responsibility for the North American portion of Time Warner's talent acquisition organization, he was blazing a new trail in an area that had been less than successful in the past. For years, corporations have tried to replace external recruiting vendors by building internal recruiting organizations and for years they failed. Recruiters would brag that the best and brightest recruiting professionals would never "go inside"—companies would never pay enough to make it worthwhile. But in the 2000s, this is no longer the case. Four key things changed to make this model sustainable:

1. Candidate acquisition became highly efficient as a result of recruiting software, resume databases, and Internet name generation techniques.

2. Companies began to *pay professional recruiters* enough money to actually attract the majority of above-average recruiters—(all *but* those who earn in the high-six and low-seven figure ranges).

3. From 2001 to 2003, the recruiting industry suffered nearly 50 percent attrition when the Internet bubble burst—great recruiting technicians were left without customers. They took their talents inside as companies ramped up talent acquisition units.

4. Candidates became more approachable. They are now willing to respond to most professional inquiries. In the past, they were inclined to respond only to recruiting

calls from big brand-name recruiting firms or prestigious boutique search firms.

Internal talent acquisition units are here to stay. They won't replace all outside recruiters, but they will definitely reduce the demand for outside providers. At Time Warner, Cormac, his boss, and his colleagues see the role as a critical cog in the overall talent management function. They are constantly evaluating the existing talent pool. They partner closely with the organization's people development unit to access talent from the standpoint of:

- *Mobility:* How easily can talent transfer among units?
- *Bench strength:* How strong is the talent depth chart against a specific position or within a particular business unit?
- *Pipeline:* How strong is the potential new employee candidate flow?

They partner with their internal talent development organization to focus on succession planning and performance measurement. It has become much more than just putting a body in a chair. They look at Time Warner across seven different operating divisions of varying size and scale to see where the gaps are going to be, what they look like, and how the gaps will impact the business. This is an enterprisewide orientation.

They also look tactically at new product direction by asking:

- What specific businesses are we getting into?
- What will the talent shortfall be?
- How can we best staff the needs?

Time Warner's cable business' foray into voice over Internet protocol (VOIP) is one tactical example. They launched 30-plus systems in 27 states. Working closely with the business leaders, they needed to:

- Identify and recruit telephone operations managers.
- Get the business to reveal talent needs.
- Avoid remolding old skill sets as a quick fix for talent needs.
- Bring in new eyes with new ideas and experiences.

As a part of this process, internal mobility issues cropped up. Every internal move had the potential of hurting one unit while helping another. That had to be balanced by the need to offer career mobility as a way of stemming attrition. Cormac explained the career mobility issue by sharing that Time Warner sees this as a major talent-related initiative. There is strong collaboration across all business units with an "employees first" attitude in regard to career mobility. They have rules of engagement to encourage cross-divisional partnership. All positions are posted on the company's intranet. Senior-level positions are circulated through a formal, internal network. When conducting a recruiting assignment, they strive to have internal employee representation in all candidate slates when possible. There is constant reinforcement that this sort of mobility is a good thing and highly encouraged.

Cormac described the talent acquisition unit this way:[2]

We constantly ask:

- Do we have the right people with the right skills sets doing the right jobs at the right time?
- Are we being proactive in our workforce planning and how much of our recruiting activity is reactive and why?

Out of this, we can decide all staffing needs and activity based on the company's needs, direction, budget, and marketplace competencies.

Organizationally we need the right people with the right skill sets. The key is to first enable management to identify the right skill sets needed ("what" and "why") in an environment of ever-changing needs and varying direction—our business is always evolving.

As far as a model for our approach, we focus on:

- Supply (turnover, retention, geography, etc.).

- Demand (can we get the talent we need, how hard, competitive landscape analysis).

- Solutions (recruiting, retention, development, etc.).

From Cormac's explanation, it certainly seems that Time Warner is on a solid track. They are perfecting the business of candidate acquisition. I hope they are also creative enough to aggressively seek the South Pole talent that will keep them competitive.

Beginning in 2001, the business of recruiting talent began a dramatic transformation and not without sizable pain. The process of how to find talent is at a crossroads. You can use both internal capabilities and external providers to get a total solution. As you set out to acquire talent, you are faced with many possibilities and situations. Let's focus on the two extremes—entry-level recruiting and recruiting for key senior leadership roles. The entry-level talent can be found at all levels including the bottom half of their academic class, the South Poler.

That Initial Leap of Faith

When it comes to campus recruiting for entry-level talent, I have heard all the horror stories from both students and those doing the recruiting. Basically, the recruiters for premier companies go to the top-tier colleges and seek out those with the highest grade point averages (GPAs)—thus actively seeking the coveted North Polers. Some are creative enough to look for an occasional academic underperformer who leads the student government or school newspaper, or who works three jobs. Undoubtedly, they have South Pole potential. By and large, however, college recruiting is a North Polers lovefest. We have previously discussed some of the reasons for this, but there is one not yet mentioned that is affectionately known as "cover your ass" (CYA). Senior management is not likely to chastise the college recruiting team if people recruited with high GPAs don't work out. However, if the recruits were South Polers—it would be much easier to blame the recruiters.

There have been some companies that run contrary to the norm. One example that I had heard about for many years is the Wall Street powerhouse Bear Stearns. Believe me, there are plenty of top academics at Bear Stearns, but they also have a creative edge for talent. Although a bit dated, the memo in the Box will give you the picture.

It sounds like Bear Stearns was made for South Polers. It's no surprise that while others on Wall Street suffered in the early 2000s, Bear Stearns knew how to zig and zag in a profitable way. Corporations don't zig and zag; people—South Polers, that is—do.

You can learn from this example. Don't let CYA hold back your recruiters. Establish a South Pole quota as a percentage of your college recruits. Select 10 percent from the pool of students with GPAs below 3.0—looking for those who are the great *communicators,* who have somehow *always stood out, who have character,* and are *passionate* and *creative.* Go ahead, take the chance—Paul Orfalea is in that crowd—it's well worth the risk—it could make or save you billions.

Memo to: All General & Limited Partners
From: Alan C. Greenberg
May 5, 1981

There has been a lot of publicity lately about firms hiring students with MBA degrees. I think it is important that we continue a policy that has helped us prosper while growing from 700 people eight years ago to over 2,600 today.

Our first desire is to promote from within. If somebody with an MBA degree applies for a job, we will certainly not hold it against them, but we are really looking for people with PSD* degrees. They built this firm and there are plenty around because our competition seems to be restricting themselves to MBAs.

If we are smart we will end up with the future Cy Lewises, Gus Levys, and Bunny Laskers. These men made their mark with a high school degree and a PSD.

*PSD stands for poor, smart and a deep desire to become rich.

Source: Alan C. Greenberg, Memos from the Chairman (New York: Workman Publishing, 1996).

They Usually Rise through Sheer Force of Will

Finding South Polers for management positions is a little easier. At this point in their career progression, South Polers have probably begun to stand out; no doubt most often having risen in the ranks from low-level jobs in collections, operations, or sales. Their achievements will have drowned out their average to below-average college GPAs. You will be comparing them to the North Polers who are also under consideration. Let me caution you. Sometimes a weak North Poler will rise in the ranks and appear to have a strong resume. Don't let the occasional empty-suit North Poler who appears to be a high achiever lure you away from the scrappy South Poler. Some North Polers who years earlier were hired into the management training program "glide path" have gotten career momentum that propelled them to higher ranks than their talent warranted. This was once dubbed the Peter Principle. Empty suits can be found in the senior ranks. But in the twenty-first century, your company may pay for this with its life. It's no longer a small matter simply solved by calling the outplacement people. How can you pick the right talent? Read on.

MANAGERS AND EXECUTIVES ARE HORRIBLE AT INTERVIEWING—I KNOW—THEY TELL ME SO

The last thing I want this book to be is a "how to" recruiting book, but I'm going to show you how to evaluate candidates during an interview using our QuickScreen™ approach. To do that, I first need to tell you how to handle the business of interviewing from top to bottom. Believe it or not, the odds are that you are *not* very good at this. Read on and be honest—you'll look at interviewing very differently after you read this material.

Would your company make an acquisition by squeezing the analysis of the deal into scraps of time during an already busy day? Would you spend millions of dollars on deals that you hastily evaluated? I hope not, but interviews are often given this sort of haphazard treatment. In this century, a new hire is a mini-acquisition and must be thoroughly analyzed.

We have been asked to scramble for yet another copy of the candidate's resume just minutes before the client is to begin interviewing. How many times does an interviewer ask, "Why am I meeting this person" just moments before the interview starts? This happens all the time. Why? Because executives and managers are many things, but professional interviewers they are not.

That's kind of amazing because managers will tell you all the time, "My people are my most important asset." If that *is* the case, than take a look at this very simple approach to successful interviewing. Some of you are going to read this and feel that I've lost my mind. You're going to feel that what I am telling you is juvenile or common sense. That's fine, but if I told you the stories that led me to feel the need to share this with you, you would be blown away.

How about the executive who interviews by spending the time talking *to* the candidate, telling him or her about the company, discussing all the things that make him or her a great and brilliant boss, and explaining the company's challenges (even for jobs that pay a quarter of a million dollars or more); this is not done as part of an interview strategy, but done as part of what I call *interview babbling*. The interview ends, the candidate is well versed in the company's issues, but the executive who is doing the hiring has little knowledge of what the candidate can bring to the party.

When we meet people as part of the hiring process, it should not be called an interview. It should be called a *preemployment knowledge exchange* (PEKE). This way, we abandon our bad interviewing habits and look at this as an exchange of information—and not just a one-sided broadcast from the interviewer.

One HR leader told me to warn candidates that the interviewer had only "one mode," which she described as "send." "Receive" was not in his repertoire. Why don't we just send in a photo of the candidate along with the resume and save everybody a lot of time? I have to share the following suggestions with you—at least some of you—but I bet every one of you who reads this learns something. Here we go—and you're welcome.

THE ART OF INTERVIEWING SCIENTIFICALLY

Get ready before you meet the candidate (review, what, how, why, identify, write). Review the person's resume and any other materials provided. The first thing I look for is job changes. A resume with a series of rapid job changes (three years or less with each employer) is a major flag to me. It can mean the person is (1) a poor performer who companies find a way to get rid of or (2) impatient and unable to invest in his or her career when put in roles that may not meet expectations. This brings me to my favorite observation about Ivy League resumes. There are two types: the one that gets to headhunters, and the one that rarely does. The one that gets to headhunters typically has a change in companies every two or, at most, three years over a 10- to 12-year period (some have 10 changes in 12 years). Unfortunately, this behavior negates all the benefits of the Ivy League credential. They are "damaged goods" of sorts. The resume reflects an attitude that they believe they should be made CEO in the first few weeks of the job. They keep moving on to places where they feel they will be better appreciated and given roles befitting their exceptional abilities. This is the pampered type that Paul Orfalea referred to earlier. The second type are the Ivy Leaguers who make their alma maters proud. They stick to their jobs, invest in their careers with an occasionally less-than-rewarding role, and rarely need a headhunter to help them land a new job. Their network and resume will do that for them.

In addition to job changes, there are other flags such as poor style and format. The resume is confusingly written or not persuasive. A resume is a sales document and most executives and managers need to be able to persuade—the resume reflects their ability to sell. There are numerous other things to look for, including:

- Discrepancies with dates.
- Their academic credentials versus your job requirements.
- Certifications.
- Titles.
- Job progression or lack thereof.
- Countless other things explained in how-to recruiting books.

Another very important measure is the candidate's compensation history. People typically earn what they are worth in the marketplace. When the resume seems to fit the senior vice president (SVP) of marketing job description you are seeking to fill at a mid-point of the salary band of $250,000, yet the candidate who submitted the resume is earning a salary of only $165,000, he or she probably won't be strong enough for the role you are filling. I often use compensation as my acid test if all else looks like a fit on paper. I rarely meet with candidates who seem to fit on paper yet have compensation that is far below the compensation for the position I am filling. There are many people with titles like senior vice president, executive vice president, chief financial officer, chief operating officer, chief executive officer, and so on, and they come in all shapes and sizes and levels of ability. Compensation almost always reflects their market value and abilities.

Candidates may rationalize this by saying their employer is underpaying them. Now let me get this straight: You work for a company, give 110 percent every day, do great things—and they don't pay your properly. And you continued to work there for five years? Either you work for a very bad company (that you chose to join) or you are not as valuable as you think you are. Either way, I have my doubts. Under the microscope you go.

Now that you have reviewed the resume and the candidate's compensation history, you need to continue to prepare. Here are seven additional steps:

1. Think about *why* you want to fill this position.
2. Think about *how* the person could fail in the role.
3. Think about *what* the person would accomplish if successful in the role.
4. Think about *what* attributes the person needs to fit into the business and get along.
5. Think about *how* the business will get in the way of this person succeeding (e.g., environment, reporting line, resources, agendas, politics, jealousy).
6. *Identify* the mission critical aspects of the job—things that must be done by this person in order for the team and the business to succeed in the first year.
7. *Write* down the questions you want to ask to measure the candidate against the issues you have just identified. That's right, *write* them down.

This line of thinking helps you focus on why you are filling this role rather than just the job description. Job descriptions are written for candidates to get a feel for the demands of the role, for HR to fit the role into the company's scheme, and for you to lay out your view of the role. They rarely reflect all aspects of the job, and hardly ever address the issue of *fit*. That is why, when you read a job description, literally hundreds or dozens of people may meet the written requirements on paper. When was the last time you had dozens of perfect candidates to choose from? You haven't—that's because the job description is not human or tangible. I would like to invent the magic algorithm that will read and score resumes to pick the perfect candidate every time. The problem is the algorithm would have to use a written input to measure the resumes against. It won't work, so we're back to interviewing.

Conducting the Interview: Don't Talk. Listen

- *Greet the person in an open manner:* Don't play head games, or use other old-school, power interview tactics.

- *Explain your approach to the interview:* Tell the candidate that you would like to *briefly* address his or her questions regarding the role and then move to a series of questions you have prepared to see how well he or she might fit what you are looking for. Explain that there will typically be a return trip during the recruiting process, at which time the candidate's questions can be fully addressed.

- *Ask the person what questions she has about the role and answer briefly.*

- *Ask your prepared questions* (more on this later) to measure the candidate against the mission critical aspects of the job. Take brief bullet-type notes.

- *Listen to the answers for the data you need and for the* way *the candidate communicates:* Does she go on and on? If so, get used to it—it won't stop after she's hired. Is she compelling? Does she communicate logically and persuasively? Do her answers seem cliché, airy, or lacking enough detail?

- *Finish the interview by letting her know she did well conveying her points to you:* You are not saying she fits, just that she did a good job presenting. Then let her know how long you think the process will take—potential next steps—and ask her level of interest so far.

- *Do NOT:*
  - Tell her you look forward to seeing her again if you don't think she fits.

—Give liberal estimates as to the hiring timeline; be conservative—expect delays.

—Delay giving feedback to the person managing the recruiting effort.

—Allow the interview to be interrupted by phone calls, e-mail, or other distractions. It's rude, unprofessional, and puts you in a bad light.

WITH EXPERIENCED PEOPLE, INTERVIEW FOR THE COMPETENCIES, NOT THE JOB DESCRIPTION

"So tell me about yourself." I'd love to meet the person who decided that question was the one to open with. When asked this question, I love to let my mind wander: "Do you *really* want me to tell you about myself (snicker, snicker)"? You need to find the actual living, breathing human beings who fit the bill. This is not done with tangential, open-ended interview questions. It's done with well-planned, competency-measuring questions. Let me explain what *competency measuring* is all about and how you can use it to ensure that you select the best talent for the role—be it a North Poler or a South Poler.

Imagine this. You are filling a role for a senior vice president of something—I don't care if it's for marketing, sales, operations, or finance—you need to measure the candidate's likelihood of success. Yes, I said measure. This all came to me by accident in the mid-1990s. (Others had written about such an approach earlier, but as a South Poler, I was not too inclined to read business books.) My newly launched firm was staffed with mostly young, inexperienced recruiters who worked behind the scenes to find the executive talent so that the senior-level consultants in our firm could evaluate them for our clients. We learned that for these young recruiters to be effective, they needed to get past the candidate's resume and dig into the person's actual competencies. Before they could evaluate the competencies, they had to know the mission critical aspects of the job and that information had to be pulled from the client.

This all led to an evaluation tool we called the *QuickScreen*[TM]. It is a critical part of our overall recruiting process called the Cornell Candidate Acquisition Model[TM] (C-CAM). It's not rocket science, but it does have rocket-scientist-like precision when it comes to selecting candidates. Basically, we get past the credentials and measure the candidate's competencies by evaluating his past experiences in very defined ways. Figure 8.1 shows where QuickScreen fits into our recruiting process and how we go about a recruiting strategy to begin with.

In Figure 8.1, there are quantitative metrics for each phase and each completed search is "back-tested" against those metrics. Figure 8.1 is an abbreviated version of a much more comprehensive flowchart found in the back of this book (pp. 197–209). As you can see, the QuickScreen happens up front in the process. We create the QuickScreen by probing the client for the *needs* behind the job description. We find out why the role is essential to the team and what key "deliverables" are expected. We find out things that are important to the client that never appear in a job description. From that, we create five to eight "Measuring Questions" that evaluate the candidate against the mission critical aspects of the job. We do this for CEO positions as well as positions in middle management.

This allows us to make better matches. Think of it this way— if you owned a football team and were recruiting for a wide receiver, the job description for wide receiver is pretty generic and does little to help you select the best fit for the role. You need to know the type of offense your team is running and the skills of your starting quarterback and the other receivers whom this person must complement.

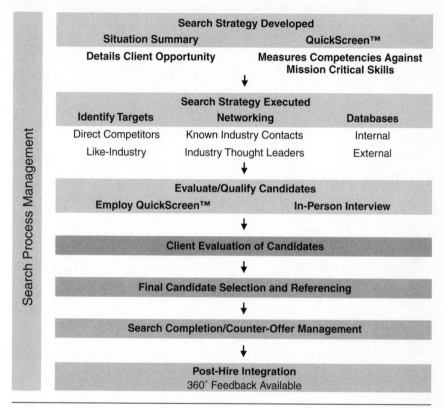

Figure 8.1   Cornell Candidate Acquisition Model: C-CAM. Our enterprisewide model—the gold standard for executive search.

Some would say that clients provide this sort of information with their list of qualifications mentioned in the typical position description. Have you read one of those lately? How about the one that says at least 15 years of finance experience required; knowledge of CRM, CPA required, and so on. I can show you about 1,000 people who fit the qualifications. Which one should you hire? Do you want to meet all 1,000 to make your choice? These types of qualifications were designed for 1960s hierarchal organizations that were not competing against a global threat operating at speeds measured in milliseconds.

The following is a sample set of QuickScreen questions designed for a client seeking a new chief technology officer (CTO). The questions are derived from our knowledge of the mission critical aspects of the job.

QuickScreen

Position	Chief Technology Officer
Client	XYZ Corp
Candidate Name	Jane Doe
Date	November 20, 2006

Mission Critical Aspects of the Position

Our client is one of the world's leading suppliers of business information, services, and research. Its database contains statistics on hundreds of millions of companies in more than two hundred countries. Our client sells that information and integrates it into software products and web-based applications. They also offer marketing information and purchasing-support services.

The CTO role is responsible for leading the technology organization under the CIO to develop new leading-edge applications, plan for the strategic growth, and manage the IT operations. The successful candidate will foster new ideas by establishing a process for innovation that allows for growth of the business. This will allow for the transformation of the IT organization from "patch and repair" to strategic forward development. Strong leadership, mentoring, and motivation will drive the initiatives for the group.

Measuring Questions

Given the mission outlined, we seek to measure some key skills, knowledge, and experiences to evaluate the candidate's likelihood of success beyond what is found on the resume. We have found that our QuickScreen approach provides an evaluation mechanism that efficiently seeks to measure the match between the candidate and the critical aspects of the position. Questions are posed to candidates as if they are currently employed—we ask candidates who are in transition to approach the questions from their most applicable former employment situation.

We ask that candidates address the following questions for this position:

1. As a member of the executive management team, your counterparts will look to you as a valued colleague helping to set cultural, technological, and operational directions for the organization. Please answer (A) and (B) and discuss specific results:

   (A) Speak to moments in your recent past where you led your organization to deploy technology to enhance business performance.

   (B) Why were the changes needed and what business, cultural, and technological barriers existed?

2. You have previously been involved in the high-level transformation of an IT organization. Give us some examples of how you took the group from "patch and repair" to strategic forward-thinking development.

3. Development of a strong, highly motivated team is critical to moving innovative initiatives forward. Please give examples of direct report employees you have successfully developed. Where are they now?

4. Today, everyone needs to do more with less. How have you implemented best practices and compliance in the technology organization?

5. As a technology leader, how have you partnered with other business unit leadership and what did you do to earn their respect as a business partner?

None of these questions say "tell me about yourself." Nor do they ask how many years' experience the candidate possesses. They probe for granular details in ways that are difficult to dodge by providing "fluff" answers. In a way, the QuickScreen is a virtual interview. It is tough, direct, and requires specific, detailed answers. If the candidate does not have the competencies, it will quickly become clear. Take Question 3 for example. It asks for specific subordinates, by name, who have gone on to achieve. If they don't have examples that you can later contact as references, they don't fit. In Question 2, if they have not led a transformation, there won't be much detail for them to offer. In many cases, candidates believe they are the perfect fit for the role until they see the QuickScreen. They often opt out of the process—which saves us countless hours and makes our process highly efficient.

How to Measure for South Pole Talent

Beyond the tangible competencies measured in the QuickScreen, there are intangible human elements: character, integrity, charm, intuitiveness, introversion, extroversion, curiosity, analytical ability, attention to detail, bias for action, perseverance, loyalty, and the like. Some of these intangibles can be measured in QuickScreen fashion as well. Consider these probing questions to measure candidates against the five South Pole characteristics:

1. *Creativity:*
   - Would those who know you best feel that you are creative and if so why?
   - Are you a practical, inside-the-box thinker, or do you feel that you think outside of the box? (Look for those who actually think "around the box"; Kathy Guarino thinks that all South Polers fit that description.)

- How do you feel about the statement: "In business, outside-the-box thinkers are often poor at execution."
- How might I measure your past creativity in business situations?

2. *Suffering or challenge:*
   - What is the most difficult personal challenge or series of challenges you have faced?
   - Do you feel you have had significant character-building experiences or have your challenges been minor ones?
   - How do you feel about this statement? "When it comes to career achievement, there are two types of people: those who have had it easy and those who have had the deck stacked against them in some way."

3. *Stood out:*
   - Can you think of a time at an early age where *you* felt that you stood out somehow? (The earlier in age the better, but exclude athletics and academics.)
   - Has this feeling of being a "standout performer" followed you throughout your life?
   - What are your *two* most significant achievements?
   - What achievements did you rank as third and fourth when you were asked to rank the top two?

4. *Communicator:*
   - Are you prone to strike up casual conversations?
   - Do you have a knack for "simplifying" difficult or confusing concepts so that others can understand more clearly? Explain.
   - Do you enjoy making presentations and why?
   - How have you performed as a member of a panel?

5. *Passionate:*
   - Are you passionate or reserved in your business dealings?

- How do you display passion when it comes to business situations?
- Do others see you as passionate or reserved?

Here is the rationale behind each of these questions:

- *Creative:* These questions allow you to open the dialogue around this topic:
  —Asking the first question from a third-person perspective is less direct and more likely to illicit more than a pat answer. It usually evokes a story that includes others and will give insight into the person as a team player as well as a creative individual. Additionally, what is important is that the person not only *feels* that they are creative but also believes that others see that characteristic in them as well.
  —The second question is for factual reinforcement of their opinion. It introduces a small bias by using the word "practical" but those who are passionate will not wilt in the face of that bias. Indeed, they may spar with you for characterizing inside-the-box thinking as practical. They not only answer the question but also make the case that outside-the-box thinking is something to be proud of.
  —The third question challenges those who have made the case that they are creative. They must now prove that they can execute as well. Obviously, almost all who are in operating roles will disagree with the statement and that will give you insight into their past accomplishments and how well they can communicate when challenged.
  —The fourth question will allow them to again give you concrete examples of past creative initiatives that attained measurable results.

- *Suffering or challenge:* Because the word suffering is a bit harsh, some South Polers will say they have not really suffered. You will need to reposition the question by letting them know you are not looking for the Abraham Lincoln sort of suffering—born in small log cabin, and so on. This line of questions is pretty straightforward. Either they do feel they have overcome challenges or they don't. Additionally, to most candidates, it is not clear as to whether there is a right or wrong answer for this. They don't know what you're probing for:

—The first question gets their list of battle scars ranked in order of pain and challenge.

—The second will tell how much they have previously reflected on the obstacles they have overcome. If there have not been many, this will not be a very spirited part of the interview. Remember, we are not looking for people who, like Abraham Lincoln, may have walked 10 miles each way to school in driving snow storms and split rails to build fences. We are looking for people who feel that they have accomplished much, yet had obstacles to overcome to do so—more than just the average obstacles faced by others who they would see as North Polers. By the way, few of these people will feel that the obstacles were huge—remember, they are resilient and they are proud of the obstacles they have overcome. But they are not complainers who see their accomplishments as anything overly special. Many will note the challenges, but will be quick to dismiss them or make light of them.

—The third question is lots of fun. This one will often have North Polers *disagreeing,* trying to say that no one truly has it easy—(a clear tip-off that the person has North Pole tendencies). However, the South Polers will immediately *agree* with the statement and probably offer some examples. Remember, they are communicators and will want to explain to you *why* their answer is the right one.

- *Stood out:* This line of questioning is pretty self-explanatory. I promise you that most South Polers will relate a story that occurs very early in life; probably before they entered their seventh year in school. Don't ask me why, but they do. We exclude athletics because the athletes will always offer up those examples first, and we won't hear the other stories that are a better measure of South Pole stand outs. The last two questions work together to build a bigger view of just how often this person feels they stood out.

- *Communicator:* If I need to explain these questions, you probably should not be reading this book. Find out if they are truly communicators. I'm talking about whether you have a communicator like a Ronald Reagan or Bill Clinton in front of you, or if you have someone less blessed in the art of communication. You need to get a clear picture of whether they are drawn to the podium or repulsed by it. The ability to simplify communications is a universal characteristic of South Polers. They are the "great explainers." They translate for others around them.

- *Passionate:* These people will be *animated* and *forward leaning* when you meet with them. They can't help it—it will show in their facial expressions, hand gestures, eye contact, and so on. So not only will the questions tell you the story, but *how* they tell you the story will tell you the story. Need I say more? I'm passionate about this.

Interviewing to evaluate South Pole characteristics is far from a science. The interviewer's knack for this is just as im-

portant as the line of questioning. Fortunately, the world of organizational psychology has matured and there are myriad
tests from all sorts of providers to evaluate more than IQ. Be
sure to put these to work for you. This field has gotten to the
point where you can't write these assessments off as "touchy-
feely" mumbo jumbo. They are real tools. They are as important as the analytical tools you use in due diligence for a
mergers and acquisitions transaction. In the twenty-first century, each hire you make is a mini-acquisition. Make no mis-
take about it.

CANDIDATES SHOULD NOT DO ANYTHING IN THE DARK THAT THEY DON'T WANT SEEN IN THE LIGHT OF DAY

Assessment testing has come a long way and is a multibillion-
dollar industry. One company, Brainbench Employment Testing, describes their personality testing product this way:

> Unlike most others, our prehire personality assessments are de-
> signed specifically for hiring. Evaluate your applicants against
> preconfigured job profiles for insight on Job-Fit, Attitude To-
> ward Work, Productivity, and Reliability.[3]

In an interview, people can indeed be fooled, but these
tests are tougher than the average interviewer. Use them to
gain added insight. They are much cheaper than making a bad
hire. My sister company, Lee Hecht Harrison, has a human
capital consulting division that can offer all sorts of tools to
test for key characteristics. The Hay Group has created the
Emotional Competency Inventory (ECI) to measure your EI
and create a plan for improvement. From this, you can build a
coaching program to remediate problem areas and expand on
positive characteristics.

There Are Many Moving Parts

We have defined the *preemployment knowledge exchange* (PEKE), formerly known as an interview, and you now know how to interview for South Pole characteristics. It is no small matter. I have explained the basics for you as an individual interviewer. I hope your organization has disciplined processes that apply to the overall strategy of interviewing. Typically, candidates will meet a group of stakeholders in the process, not a single individual. There should be a plan for how this group obtains the knowledge needed to assess the candidates. I presented this process as one-on-one, but in reality it is a series of one-on-ones as part of a team of evaluators and stakeholders. Other books can give you chapter and verse on all this.

Additionally, remember that before you can achieve world-class recruitment prowess, you must have an employee friendly organization, convey that message through employee branding, and become strong practitioners in the science of recruiting. That is the science behind:

- Casting the net for candidates.
- Evaluating those candidates through effective interviewing and assessment tools.
- Convincing the chosen candidate that your opportunity is career enhancing enough to make a move.
- Successfully integrating the candidate into the organization, which is where talent deployment and recruiting overlap.

Congratulations, you now have all the talent you were hoping for. What do you do now?

9

☆☆ Evaluate ☆☆ and Deploy

Matching the Talent to the Mission and the Team

The wrong person in the job can be more costly than leaving the chair empty.

—Alan Guarino

The Human Capital Institute offers a course toward an accredited professional designation called *human capital strategist.* In its first 18 months of existence, the Institute has attracted 35,000 members offering "communities by region," shared learning programs, online and offsite training, thought-leader panels online, and a host of other industry-changing initiatives. The demand for a strategist designation in human capital is a clear sign of how important talent management really is to our business survival. The cliché "Our people are our most important asset" has been around for years, but at the same time, we spent more money recruiting replacements than we did training those employees we had. Actions speak louder than words. So let's look at talent deployment—the art of matching the talent to the mission—which is easier said than done. The mission is constantly changing and so must the mix of the talent deployed. This is a very dynamic process. You need a diverse pool of talent properly deployed.

No Blood and Guts, No Glory: A Talent Deployment Case Study

The following quotes were made by a very successful individual from the past century:

- "If everybody is thinking alike, then somebody isn't thinking."
- "Do your damnedest in an ostentatious manner all the time."
- "I don't measure a man's success by how high he climbs but how high he bounces when he hits bottom."
- "Never tell people how to do things. Tell them what to do and they will surprise you with their ingenuity."
- "We herd sheep, we drive cattle, we lead people. Lead me, follow me, or get out of my way."
- "A good plan today is better than a perfect plan tomorrow."
- "Courage is fear holding on a minute longer."
- "Accept the challenges so that you can feel the exhilaration of victory."
- "I do not fear failure. I only fear the 'slowing up' of the engine inside of me which is pounding, saying, 'Keep going, someone must be on top, why not you?' "
- "CONQUER!"

Maybe you're thinking it's some great corporate leader, an Andrew Carnegie or Jack Welch? It sounds a bit like our old friend Henry Ford, too. Perhaps it's some great emotional leader, the founder of some self-empowerment movement, or even a great world leader like Theodore Roosevelt or Sir Winston Churchill.

These words are indeed from one of the most remarkable and most successful people of the past hundred years. Coming from another West Pointer who was close to being the Goat of his class, they are the words of General George S. Patton. Ironically, Patton is best known today for a quote he probably never uttered: The line from the movie starring

George C. Scott about how Patton beat Erwin Rommel in the desert after reading the great German tank commander's book. Actually, Rommel never wrote a book on tank warfare, but he did write one about the infantry. Having received the General George S. Patton Award during graduation from West Point in 1982, I have a special affinity for the general. But was Patton's talent truly suited for combat? Did he always fit the mission?

Patton struggled at West Point, and he dropped out after a year or so of his first try. But he came back. How many people have the drive and courage to do that? You get drummed out, humiliated—you're even *lower* than the Goat, since the Goat is still at the Academy. But Patton wasn't really stupid. He was dyslexic, which was practically unknown, certainly by the layperson, back when he was attending the U.S. Military Academy. I contend that many, if not most South Polers are dyslexic or are afflicted with attention deficit disorder, but that will need to be the topic of another book. Patton overcame it though, like he did everything else. He confronted his disability head on. It has been said that as a young officer after graduating, not yet having faced live ammunition in battle, he had the lingering suspicion that he might be a coward when it came to actual battle conditions. How do you prove something like that to yourself in peacetime? The folklore (and probably truth) is that Patton went out to his army base's practice rifle range and stood up between a couple of targets while target practice with live ammo was underway, just so he could gauge his reactions. Not surprisingly, he passed with flying colors.

That's not the kind of test you're ever going to get from the IQ people. But Patton knew what he was doing. He knew better than his superiors where he needed to test himself. He also knew that being a successful leader of men required both book knowledge and a certain savvy.

This is precisely the kind of savvy, self-reliant (and perhaps even a little risky) behavior that talented South Polers often exhibit. The North Polers have not typically had to stick their necks out. They're accustomed to doing most everything by the book, simply because they're good at it and never get in trouble that way. The South Polers have generally "failed" when they try to follow the rules or have even been humiliated. Some are actually kicked out of school. The South Polers are forced to find alternative ways to succeed. This usually makes them more maverick than the North Polers and highly inventive. If necessity is the mother of invention, South Polers have to be pretty inventive to reach success through the back alleys.

Eventually, Patton saw his first combat action, under the command of Blackjack Pershing. They were down on the Mexican border, looking for the bandit Pancho Villa, who'd been raiding U.S. towns. Patton came by his western-style pearl-handed revolvers honestly. He was probably in on the last Wild West action in history.

When Pershing was placed in charge of all the American forces going to Europe during World War I in 1917, Patton went along with him. Oddly, Patton never got to see much action during World War I. He was put in charge of a new-fangled contraption that the army wanted to try. It was called a tank and at that time was a pretty ugly, ungainly piece of machinery—not very battle-worthy at all. But Patton became very passionate about the tank. He had the native instinct to see its potential, which was soon to transform modern warfare. So he and his men rode around in some field in France in these odd machines, which tipped over and got overheated. Then the war was over.

World War II was different. Patton almost immediately sprang into action, getting the army to set up a tank training facility out West to prepare the new generation of U.S. tank commanders and crews. Patton instinctively knew that in this war, the tank's time had come. The U.S. tanks of that time were still rather comical. Their profile was too high, and their turrets didn't swivel. (Patton came up with the idea for a new swiveling turret for U.S. tanks.) Meanwhile, in North Africa, Field Marshal Erwin Rommel's gas-powered Panzers were having a field day with the British. The German tanks were far superior to anything the Allies had. Furthermore, Rommel was an expert on tank battle tactics. The Germans specialized in "massing" firepower, while the Americans and British still thought the name of the game was one-on-one tank battles. Rommel, like Robert E. Lee, was the classic North Poler superstar type, accustomed to dominating the opposition by sheer force of intellect—until, that is, the Nazis coerced him into committing suicide, which didn't look quite so smart.

Patton and his first tank crews arrived in North Africa in 1942 and promptly suffered one of the worst drubbings in the war at the hands of Rommel's superior forces in Kasserine Pass.

General Bernard Montgomery was the commander of Allied forces in North Africa and British troops in Egypt were pushing the Germans west when Patton arrived for Operation Torch. Patton's orders were to win the French in Morocco over to the Allied side, then use Tunisia as a base to assist the British in the Libyan desert. The ultimate goal was to make the Mediterranean safe for Allied shipping.

So Rommel in November of 1942 found himself pincered between U.S. forces to the west and British forces to the east. Tactical genius that he was, the commander of the *Deutches Afrikakorps,* spearheaded by the formidable Panzer divisions, was able to keep both forces at bay. Then came the Battle of Kasserine Pass. The U.S. forces, and in particular its tanks, were crushed by the Germans.

Almost any other general would probably have resigned his command, but Patton was long accustomed to setbacks in his life, accustomed to having to learn things the hard way. Patton possibly was even grateful to Rommel for teaching him a valuable lesson. It was a painful tutorial, to be sure, but Patton and the U.S. Army used the lessons learned to great effect for the rest of the Africa campaign and the war. The U.S. Army drastically altered the command and control of its tank divisions and began to coordinate with air cover. The results were almost immediate. The Americans repelled Rommel the next time they met, pushing his forces back through that very same Kasserine Pass and, soon, out of North Africa altogether. On May 12, 1943, the remaining Axis forces in Africa surrendered. The West Point South Poler had kicked some serious butt by being smart, inventive, and persistent—just *smart* would not have been *enough*.

George S. Patton had taken his own advice: "I don't measure a man's success by how high he climbs but how high he bounces when he hits bottom." There might not be a better definition of the valuable South Poler. It is said that some people have a hard time coping with success. Maybe so, but it's still much easier than coping with failure. It takes a special type of person to be able to recoup after a major setback. And for those who have little or possibly even no experience in adversity, it's especially difficult. There is clearly a need to match the talent to the mission. And Patton's superiors, Pershing, Bradley, and Ike, had done so with him.

You probably thought I was writing about Patton, but I was really writing about Blackjack Pershing, Omar Bradley, and Dwight Eisenhower. Pershing, as Patton's boss, matched him to the mission of figuring out if tanks could be useful in future combat. Bradley and Eisenhower matched him against the *Deutches Afrikakorps* knowing that the United States was outgunned, outmanned, and facing challenges that a more academic, calculating leader might chose to retreat from. The magic of all this is that our army had the diversity of talent to deploy in varied situations. We did not have a homogeneous talent pool of leaders—we had thinkers, doers, scrappers, artists, and down-right courageous talent for just about any mission the dynamic state of war could throw at us. Long before we had human capital strategists, we had military leaders who were strategizing, acquiring, developing, deploying, retaining, and evaluating. Now that business is war, what do you think we need to do? One option would be to ask the Human Capital Institute.

The Right Talent for the Job

Many of our modern athletes can be divided into two types of high achievers, which we recognize almost immediately. There is the super-talented, pampered physical specimen, and then there is the never-back-down, highly driven scrapper. Guess which group is from the North Pole and which is from the South Pole? A football player like Terrell Owens has been winning sports since high school. Although he faced big challenges in his life outside sports, he seems to have breezed through every athletic activity he pursued. It came easy to him—he's a natural. In no way do I want to pick on Owens; he simply provides one side of an important analogy to contrast North Pole versus South Pole attributes. In a sense, you can't blame him for acting spoiled. He was probably spoiled by every coach and person he's ever met in his meteoric career. By the time he got to college, he was walking down a red carpet everywhere he went. Now take a player like Donavan McNabb. Here's a guy whose talent has been questioned almost every step of the way. It seems like he's forever playing with an injury.

He's even got Rush Limbaugh on his back. You can't get any more oppressed than that. But McNabb shrugs it all off (including the circus surrounding Owens) and keeps playing hard and winning.

I'm not saying don't hire the Terrell Owenses. Their talent is very real and might even be worth the trouble they cost you. But don't *forget* about the Donovan McNabbs. They may not be as glamorous, but they're often even more productive, especially over the long haul, and they are usually much easier to get along with. Let me put it to you this way: You're about to go into action in North Africa against Erwin Rommel's *Afrikakorps*—who would you rather have as your commander, Donovan McNabb or Terrell Owens? That's a no-brainer.

But here's another hypothetical. You're putting together a team for the Olympics and you need a great sprinter. Who do you choose, Donovan McNabb or Terrell Owens? Obviously, you go with Owens, despite the hell he puts you through. The Olympics is an example of an arena where sheer talent typically carries the day. There's a reason the gold medal is given for winning and not for second place. Some businesses or business situations are oriented this way, and they may need the gifted super-scholar. But it's a rare business that needs only North Polers. And very often it is the talented South Poler who puts the team in a position to win.

Terrell Owens wasn't born a great wide receiver. There have been many little people throughout his career who have helped, instructed, and facilitated him. Even Terrell Owens is the product of a team. This brings me to another important point about North and South Polers. North Polers can have a tendency to think they made it entirely on their own. He or she may look down at his or her team members— and there's nothing more demoralizing to a team than that. The successful South Poler is more likely to give credit to those on his or her team, those who helped along the way. And this is a great morale builder for the team (more on this later). You have to be able to consider not only what a player adds, but what he or she might *detract* from a team. It's the bottom line that ultimately counts for any business, after all. The Philadelphia Eagles finally realized that Terrell Owens was costing them more than he was helping them. It was a painful decision, but one they came to the hard way—just as a South Poler would.

So match the talent to the mission, and consider the need for team players. I was recently enlightened by a very simple observation from a professor in the department of behavior science and leadership at West Point, where I was asked to present to a class as a visiting executive; at lunch, we discussed this book and one of the professors summed it up this way— "academics is a worthy pursuit—but it is *not* a team sport." Most business leadership roles require team players. George Bradt, author of the book *Hot Landings: Succeeding in the Most Challenging New Leadership Roles,* told me: "Alan, in our program we spend one day focusing on the leader that we are assisting; the rest of the time we focus on the team. Leaders don't fail directly—their teams fail." Very interesting, George— you're right.

The Rock-Bottom Line

We are going to need all kinds of amazing talent to remain competitive and that talent needs to fit the mission. Once we've planned, but we don't acquire the talent, the other parts of the talent management process won't matter.

Too often in modern business, and in particular in entry- and mid-level corporate recruiting, the overriding quality we pay attention to is academic achievement. But making the match is much more delicate than that. Brains, as we have been exploring, are not the only quality that makes someone successful. Intelligence is just the easiest desirable quality to measure. Give a test and pick the top scorers. It's easier for the recruiter really. Just read the test scores. How do you measure determination? How do you measure loyalty? How do you measure industriousness?

Not every corporate job requires a rocket scientist. If you're locked in a race to the moon with the Soviet Union, sure, hire the brainiest college professors you can dig up. But most of the time, the situation calls not for a degree in astrophysics but for someone who has excellent social, decision-making, people-reading, or great organizational skills. Or someone who's simply more determined than the other guy. Leaders rarely require the same technical brilliance found in their most valuable subordinates.

Increasingly, the business world is beginning to realize that there's more to be on the lookout for than a high GPA. The term *South Polers* lumps together all those skills that are hard to pin down with a test. This book, I hope, helps to explain why a company may need to hire a Ulysses S. Grant and not a Robert E. Lee or, better yet, to hire both. I hope I've shown you that there is often great untapped potential in the folks at the bottom half of their academic class who are often a great fit when building a team. South Polers need to be hired at all levels of the company. They need to be put in charge of divisions—hired into management training programs—put in charge of project teams—and basically cultivated as we have done for decades with their more scholarly North Pole counterparts. Cultivate South Polers, don't rely on Adam Smith to propel you to success. With global competition, we have not the time to waste. Make the match.

THERE ARE TOOLS TO HELP YOU MAKE THE MATCH

Thanks to modern academic study, organizational psychologists have created many vehicles for talent assessment. These tools allow you to delve into a person's psyche to evaluate how they need to be led or what kind of leader they are. The tests create a psychological profile to define the individual. When creating teams, you need the proper mix of individuals. A team of leaders will be ineffective—no one will follow. A team of linear thinkers will lack creativity. Matching the talent to the mission can be much more empirical than the gut-feeling decision making used by the likes of Henry Ford, Ike Eisenhower, or J.P. Morgan.

A few years ago, I was looking for an assessment tool that could predict the likelihood that a candidate would succeed in the position we were recruiting for. That's when I learned about a testing approach that was explained as *reverse behavioral assessment*. The concept is pretty logical. If you are filling a position that already has others in the same role, you can assess those who are already highly successful in the role. This testing provides the assessment company with a "motivational profile" of the people who are successful in the role. Once this profile is developed, the assessment firm can design a test to identify individuals who match the profile of the already proven achievers. Some assessment companies can create these tests from a sample of as few as five individuals. Suffice it to say that matching the talent to the mission is the critical element of successful talent deployment.

With the talent on board and deployed in your organization, you need to constantly develop and improve performance. There are countless ways to approach this and you will be amazed at the creativity that is at work.

10

☆ ☆ Deploy Cutting-Edge ☆ ☆
Methods for
Staff Development

Invest in Human Capital

*We spend much more on recruiting than on talent development—
that has to change.*

—Alan Guarino

It amazes me that we hire people and, for the most part, we then just *hope* they will succeed. A famous athletic coach said, "Hope is not a strategy!" Yet for most businesses, hope is indeed the company's staff development strategy. Businesses do spend money on training and development, but they are not given anywhere near the investment they deserve, and companies often buy the wrong things. The *right* investments in talent development must be made. You don't think it will pay off? You don't think you can find the money in your budget? Keep thinking like that and you're in big trouble.

In the early-1940s through the mid-1960s, if you asked CFOs how much their companies spent on technology, they would probably reference their phone bills. Their biggest technological expenses would have been the money spent on telecommunications, not on computers. Who needs computers? What is a computer? We're a consulting company, law firm, or newspaper; we're not sending anyone to the moon—why would we need a computer? The investment in talent is now at the same point where the investment in technology was in the early-1970s. Businesses and organizations need to take the leap and get serious about investing in talent. Not just holding training classes, but really investing in talent. I know you go back to those nagging little questions—where will the money come from? What will the payoff be? The same questions were asked about making an investment in technology.

When businesses transformed from manual processes to automation, many believed it was money ill-spent. The old, stubby pencil worked just fine—who needs a spreadsheet? It took courage to take the leap. Here's a real-life example.

In the late 1980s and early 1990s, The Bank of New York and Banker's Trust Company were engaged in a serious competition for supremacy in securities processing. Securities processing is the business on Wall Street that keeps track of stock trades, moves securities, and money, and basically provides the back-office services needed for the brokerage industry to function. From the customer's perspective, the glaring difference between Banker's Trust and The Bank of New York was always about the technology. Banker's Trust appeared to have invested far more and was very successful at winning the higher-margin accounts, maintaining a more sophisticated look and feel to the business. When Deutsche Bank bought Banker's Trust, it appeared that their technology investments had paid off. Both Banker's Trust and The Bank of New York made the transformation by spending large sums of money on technology in business units that had been highly manual.

The point here is that the previous generation of management probably could not have fathomed getting a return on that sort of expenditure. If you told them that their successors would need to budget millions on technology, they would have told you it was impossible. They would have said the company does not have the finances to make such expenditures—it simply could not afford to invest in such major technology initiatives. Who could ever imagine that the IT budget could be in the millions or billions for that matter? No company could afford that.

But companies made the investment, and the return was exceptional. Organizations now need to make the same sort of investment in talent optimization, and they will be rewarded through the increased productivity of the people in whom they invest. You need to find the money; and you need to spend it on the talent you employ to make your company better, and better, and better every day. Why not spend as much money on training and development as you do on recruitment? That would be a major shift. Your talent would be the best in your business and you would be poised to win. Talk to a smart CFO and find the money to make this bet.

Mistakes can be made in talent development, just as mistakes were made in technology investments. We have all heard of the $100 million technology project that was scrapped and never made it to full deployment. The same can happen in the world of talent development. The development efforts must be in line with the business's strategy and the individual's development needs. Within those guidelines, there is much that managers can do to increase the productivity of their organizations. Talent development resources range from seminars on leadership to individual coaching from outside coaches hired by the business to work one-on-one with employees. The human resources (HR) division of the company should drive these initiatives just as the CIO has driven the technology resources in line with the needs of the business unit. It must be a partnership between the business unit and HR so that the best results are achieved. There is a lot of training material out there to buy and not all of it is good. In this chapter, we look at a few of the most innovative offerings on the market.

PEAK PERFORMANCE IS MORE THAN A PHRASE

If you think you know about all the training and development tools that are in the market, I challenge you to tell me about a little boutique firm called Apex Performance. "It is a one of a kind, scientific approach for enhancing performance that utilizes advanced sensory feedback technologies to train and measure improvement of five 'inner' competencies that separate good performers from great performers,"[1] says this specialized training company that helps businesses optimize the talent on their team. Apex hooks your staff members up to machines with wires and helps them transform their behaviors. This is the cutting-edge stuff of Olympic athletes in training and was first developed at West Point in a biofeedback lab to help cadets perform better in athletics and other aspects of cadet life.

Anyone can perform well when everything is going just right and conditions are favorable. But what about when conditions are unfavorable and things are going against you, when the pressure is on to deliver your best? Who can really deliver then? The answer, according to Apex, is those who can truly control their emotional and physiological responses to the stressors. Retired Colonel Louis Csoka and his colleagues at Apex, develop talent by putting employees into a training environment designed to integrate the latest sensory feedback technologies with mastering the peak performance competencies.

Csoka explains that people carry around images of themselves, of who they are and how they perform. Most of this self-image is determined by our thoughts (positive and negative) and maintained and reinforced with our self-talk. Given the negativism surrounding many people's lives, being positive and having trust and confidence in our ability is really hard work. Recognizing that people need to take responsibility for their cognitions (thoughts) about work, performance, and life in general and providing training that helps them achieve it is what the peak performance approach is all about. There is scientific evidence for the effectiveness of positive thinking training and Apex has an innovative way of using affirmations as a primary tool for transforming negative thoughts into positive ones and pessimism into optimism.

Traditional talent development solutions have not produced the expected results in performance improvement and productivity increases. Nonbusiness organizations have met with much greater success in applying peak performance techniques for enhancing performance. Elite athletes have demonstrated, for decades, the relationship between their success and the mental training aspect of their preparation. The time has come for businesses to embrace this science-based development approach. It's the cutting-edge. Take a closer look at how it works in a corporate setting.

A Business Case Study

During a dinner conversation in Gettysburg, the CEO of a *Fortune* 500 healthcare company and Louis Csoka were talking about their pasts. As Csoka described the founding of West Point's Performance Enhancement Center and the program he created in 1989, the CEO's interest and curiosity was peaked. As a result, the first-ever Peak Performance Center and program in a major corporation was born. The company created a Development Center with three fully equipped training rooms that housed the sensory feedback technologies that are an essential part of the peak performance training. The first participants in the program were:

- The CEO and his executive team
- Twelve high-potential managers
- Members of the HR team

Subsequent cohorts of business leaders were selected based on their critical positions and immediate business challenges.

The program consisted of 25 hours of one-on-one training and coaching in the five peak performance competencies:

1. Goal setting
2. Positive/effective thinking
3. Stress and energy management
4. Attention control and visualization and imagery

A typical schedule would have the executives in the training rooms twice a week for an hour each. Participants were required to practice the skills they were learning between sessions. Progress was monitored on a daily basis with periodic checks to measure change in behavior and/or performance.

Significant improvements were achieved in the development of all of the peak performance competencies, changes in behavior and performance, and business success indicators. Figure 10.1 displays the degree of improvement in peak per-

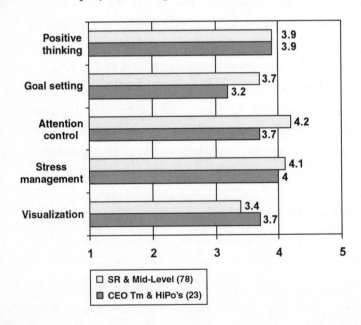

Figure 10.1   Improvements in peak performance competency (Apex).

formance competencies. The scale ranges from *No Improvement (1)* to *Significant Improvement (2)*.

One of the indicators of the power of the training was actual change in behavior and performance by the participants. Figure 10.2 shows the improvements in key behaviors and in performance.

Once mastered, these competencies become skills that carry an individual through life's struggles and challenges with greater levels of optimism, confidence, focus and concentration, as well as a sense of calmness, control, and overall self-mastery.

Knowing about Peak Performance and Louis Csoka's work provides much to consider as you develop your critical talent—the talent that is within yourself and within your team. We waste a lot of money making "bad hires," but most bad hires

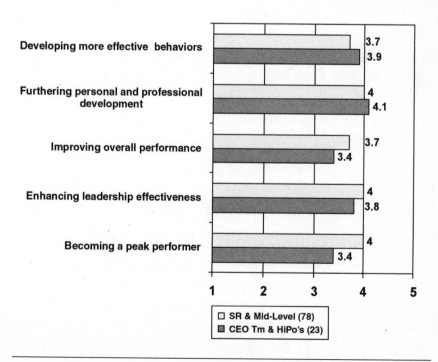

Figure 10.2   Improvements in key behaviors (Apex).

are not really bad hires; they are just bad starts that never get off the launch pad.

How about a Hot Landing for Executives in a New Position?

When I was introduced to George Bradt, I was certain I had met the inventor of "executive on-boarding." Bradt is CEO of a company called PrimeGenesis. He eats, breathes, and sleeps the topic. There was no question in my mind that when it came to getting new employees off to a winning start, George Bradt thought of everything. No matter how well your selection or promotion process is, people beginning new roles have an integration cost that can be measured by how quickly the person begins delivering results. Quick, high-quality results are the desired outcome, but rarely happen. That is where a "Hot Landing" comes in. By investing in a professional approach to integrating new employees at the management level and above, a company can see a great return-on-investment. George Bradt explains his firm's approach and the value of a formal 100-day plan for individuals assuming new management roles as needing to match transition tools to the situation.

Matching Transition Tools to the Situation

Today's job transitions are more rapid, unsettling, and varied than ever. The good news is that there is an increased array of helpful tools and resources as depicted in Figure 10.3. The more complex the situation and orientation and the more urgent the transition, the more intrusive the intervention should be. Internal mentors are the least intrusive

Senior leaders	**Mentoring** Generally internal and informal	**Transition Coaching** Personal advice and counsel for leader	**Transition Acceleration** Experience-based help for team across key tasks
	Knowledge Sharing on the job	**Leadership Development** behind the scenes	**Jumpstart Team Performance** in the room, with the team
Assistance provided	Network access Moral support Communication	Advice and counsel Scenario planning Role playing for practice	Drive better results faster Hands-on work on strategy, people, and culture
Authority	Company knowledge	Process knowledge	Operational experience
Situation	Stable	Mixed	Unsettled
Orientation	Promoted in place	"Internal" transfer	New to company culture
Urgency	Time to learn	Balanced	Acute need to act

Figure 10.3 Tools for the task (PrimeGenesis; G. Bradt).

and appropriate when all that the new leader needs is on-the-job knowledge sharing. The next step up is transition coaching where behind-the-scenes leadership development is useful. George Bradt explained that in Hot Landings, PrimeGenesis handles these few, most complex situations where hands-on, operationally experienced transition accelerators may be necessary.

Analogies may be helpful here. Professional golfers have coaches and caddies. Their coaches serve as behind-the-scenes advisors between tournaments. Their caddies, like harbor pilots, white water rafting guides, operating room nurses, and mountain-climbing sherpas, certainly do provide advice and counsel, but their real value is in their on-the-course, in-the-boat, in-the-room, and on-the-mountain tangible contributions. They accelerate progress through what they do as well as what they say. In the most complex transitions, that extra leverage can make all the difference.

Bradt's firm, PrimeGenesis, is an executive on-boarding and transition acceleration group that helps leaders in new and challenging positions deliver better results faster and reduce the risk of failure. They provide hands-on facilitation of practical tools based on their own senior line management and organizational development experience with leading companies around the world. For Hot Landings clients, that help is often the difference between failure and astounding success. Robert Rigby-Hall, the global head of HR at Lexis Nexis explains it this way:

> For both new hires and senior level internal promotions it's key that they start delivering results quickly—the long "honeymoon" periods are over, and people expect to see results fast. The process that we have used at LexisNexis with the help of PrimeGenesis has given us close to 100 percent success rate with these individuals. It has meant that they hit the ground running on Day 1 with the confidence that they truly understand their stakeholders' needs and what they need to deliver.[2]

BEYOND THE HOT LANDING—CONTINUAL PERFORMANCE ENHANCEMENT

The care and feeding of the talent pipeline is one of the critical tasks for organizations as the war for talent heats up again due to global demographic trends and increasing pressure for innovation and continual productivity increases. My colleagues at our sister company, Lee Hecht Harrison, have a global talent solutions business, headed by Kevin Gagan. They develop leaders who can drive consistency and results-based execution while at the same time developing a tolerance for paradox and ambiguity.

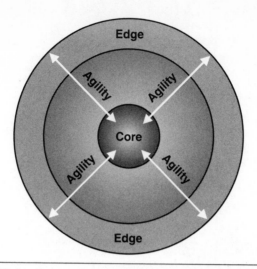

Figure 10.4   Core, edge, and agility (Lee Hecht Harrison).

Talent Solutions built the framework in Figure 10.4 from their research with over 130 senior clients who wanted to prepare leaders with the capability to gather broad intelligence, gain rapid insight, accelerate decision making, and enhance their ability to communicate and take action. To have maximum impact, they focus on developing agility at four leadership talent tipping points—the four key career stages: emerging, core, accelerated, and legacy—as shown in Figure 10.5.

Approaches for Developing Agility

To develop agility at each of these stages requires corresponding organizational levels of investment and commitment, such as the following approaches:

- *Emerging:* Self-initiated modules that present broad issues to introduce employees to the broader environmental context of their industry. Self-assessment quizzes and

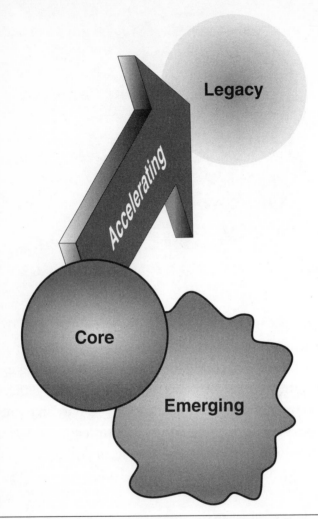

Figure 10.5   Tipping points (Lee Hecht Harrison).

short single point learning modules that introduce self-awareness concepts.

- *Core:* Introduction of basic techniques of agility, selection of focus from case studies, building consistency in general management competencies.

- *Accelerating:* Targeted development for identified successors, high potentials, and subject matter experts. Using simulations, coaching, and group learning environments to approach current business challenges in complex environments. Using Fast Feedback Leadership™ to respond to groups of employees.

- *Legacy:* Tapping extensive experience to create case studies from experience and mentoring of key successors through complex situations. Bridging generational differences through getting to shared strategic outcomes versus focusing on process difference.

Agility Drives Innovation

Lee Hecht Harrison's, *Fast Feedback Leadership* process (Figure 10.6) supports leaders with continuous data from the organization, gathered in interactive "pulses." This data is automatically harvested using an interactive platform of predictive metrics and online interactive communication, allowing leaders to coach their organization to drive change, confirm strategic alignment, and increase business results. I explain this in greater detail later.

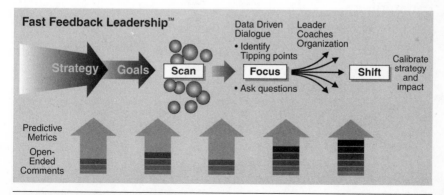

Figure 10.6   Fast Feedback Leadership (Lee Hecht Harrison).

Their Fast Feedback Leadership process provides leaders with the tools to be agile, look broadly, focus behaviors and actions on areas that need attention, and shift when they need to increase maximum impact, making change happen.

Fast Feedback Accelerates Leadership Learning

Lee Hecht Harrison takes a very different approach to developing leaders—not just coaching executives—and giving them feedback about their competencies and performance; they help executives get off the couch and coach their organizations. Fast Feedback Leaders are prepared to use feedback *from* the organization to create data-driven dialogues.[3] This is more than presenting data, asking for ideas, and making an action plan. Fast Feedback enables leaders to enter an online and in-person dialogue where both the manager and employees are willing to examine their own assumptions, see beyond current solutions, and change. When employees have given their feedback and leaders take action, a cycle of trust and engagement is fostered. Research shows that this leads to an organizational climate of productivity and performance.[4] The ability to question current practices sets up an environment alive with intelligence, where people become energized and managers gain commitment.

This is not communication on steroids—where messages are broadcast to the organization, but an interactive approach that leaders are using to listen to the people in their organizations, tapping into an open source of intelligence. Leading interactively involves using Fast Feedback to kick off a data-driven dialogue with groups in the organization to gain greater clarity for action.[5] Leaders can then use this clarity to coach their organizations, mobilizing and focusing employee's efforts.

Conclusion

The examples in this chapter shed light on the level of creativity and science that can be applied to talent development. Most development boils down to some form of training, but not those old-school classes or canned off-site seminars. Development is dynamic and ongoing. It needs to be woven into the workings of the business in many different and innovative ways.

11

☆ ☆ Lead ☆ ☆

Follow Me and Do as I Do

Keep away from people who try to belittle your ambitions. Small people always do that, but the really great make you feel that you, too, can become great.

—Mark Twain

You've assembled a great team of North and South Polers in your organization, and you are developing them to the peak of their potential. What do you do now? Well, there is no substitute for leadership—not talent, or luck. Great businesses are led by confident leaders who can inspire confidence and promote a winning corporate culture.

Lead, Follow, or Get Out of the Way

My colleague Steve Harrison is writing a book on leadership and was astute enough to consider looking at the teachings of West Point. I believe that West Point is the premier leadership training institution in the United States—perhaps the world. When the United States moved from conscription (the draft) to an all-volunteer army, leaders needed to understand and become competent in positive approaches to leadership. To this day, many civilians believe that army leadership is about giving orders to people who have to follow them. That could not be farther from the truth. Army leadership is about many things, the least of which is giving orders.

Here is a quick overview that is relevant to corporate leadership science. In the early-1970s, it is safe to say that the U.S. military was a severely damaged institution. Some say it had lost its integrity, its cohesive *esprit' d corps,* and a clear view of its mission. But thanks to the pendulum theory, things were destined to swing back if the initiative was taken. And so it was. There was much emphasis placed on honor education—teaching ethics and integrity in a very practical way, at all levels. In the 1970s, the military was getting what we now believe the corporate world is in dire need of in the 2000s—a dose of ethics.

At the same time, the military was teaching a concept called *positive leadership*. It was a concept that challenged leaders to learn to *inspire* others to perform their duties. It was about motivating people to perform through positive reinforcement rather than through threats of punishment. I think the most important leadership concept was embodied in the teachings of something called *commander's intent*. This leadership concept is the basis for empowering decision making at the lowest levels of the organization. If the staff understands what the leader intends to do and what the strategy is, as well as the tactics, then, in the face of problems or obstacles, they can make their own decisions and further the mission even if the tactics were not those specifically directed by the leader. We called this *power down*. The military did not want a hierarchal, dictatorial leadership climate. They wanted decision making at all levels, by bright soldiers, who understood the mission and the commander's intent so those soliders could make decisions in the absence of specific orders.

Not surprisingly, this is also where the military felt the enemy was vulnerable. The military believed that the Soviet's heavy command-and-control structure left them easy prey if the United States attacked their leadership elements. To simplify the assertion, the army felt if they took out the Soviet's command elements, the rank-and-file soldier would pull off the road and surrender. If the soldiers were not truly committed to the mission and not clear about the commander's intent, how could they fight? They couldn't! Leadership is about empowering decision making at the lowest possible levels and creating a culture of inspired individuals who know where the company is going.

Inspire Others to Greatness

In the business world, we have the challenge of leading people. I bet there are more books on this topic than there are on religion. I'd like to expose you to a leadership approach that South Polers and North Polers will thrive under. This approach, *transformational leadership,* will help you "power down."

Transformational leadership makes things happen and builds on the ability to inspire. Leadership theory is a heavily played topic, and there are old concepts, such as the trait theory and others, but I encourage you to investigate transformational leadership.

First You Must Possess a Vision

Vision is what makes a leader passionate, and enables him or her to then carry that enthusiasm to the role as leader. Without a vision, there is no transformational leader. Let me give you an example: When Tom Glocer took the helm of the renowned media company Reuters in July 2001, he entered at a time when the stock was poised to crash. Financial services firms had cut back dramatically on their spending, which hurt Reuters, and their technology needed an overhaul. It was the perfect storm of sorts. Politics was also stacked against Glocer; he was a young American running a long-standing European company. Not only that, he was a mergers and acquisitions attorney and not a journalist; a situation that many felt was not going to work. A well-known Reuters competitor benefited from a cartoon in the *Financial Times* that showed Reuters' stock declining during Glocer's first year while the competitor's stock had climbed.

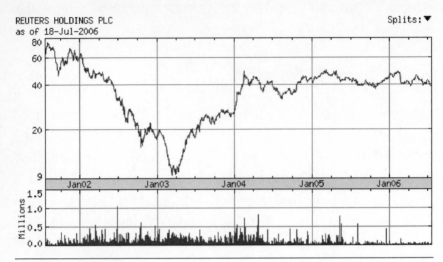

Figure 11.1   Reuters holdings PLC stock graph.

Fast-forward three years (Figure 11.1) and there is a much different story. Reuters' stock was reversed as of the first quarter of 2003 after it bottomed. Up from a low of close to $9 per share to the high $30 range by this book's publication, Reuters has rocketed under Glocer's transformational leadership. Glocer accomplished this by first establishing a vision and then launching a five-year business strategy that he dubbed "Fast Forward." Although it has not yet regained its all time high, the results of the successful transformation are clear.

My friend John Sadowsky of Mosaic Capital and his colleague Loïck Roche, both management professors at Grenoble Ecole de Management, in their paper "Leadership Best Practice: Providing a Sense of Deeper Purpose,"[1] present a great narrative on the way transformational leaders can get people to see and *feel* the vision. (See the Box on pp. 185–186.)

If you recall my earlier discussion about employee branding, this Macintosh story also illustrates that special ability for entrepreneurial companies to create a sense of belonging that larger companies must now pursue if they are to have a success-

In his book, *Culture Jam,* Kalle Lasn argues that the most powerful narcotic in the world is the promise of belonging. This "narcotic" increases dramatically in power if the leader can provide the group with a unique identity and convince the members that they are somehow different and special. One of the masters of this motivational dynamic was Steve Jobs of Apple Computer, who told a unique story of identity to his Macintosh team in the early 1980s. Bennis and Biederman (1997) describe Jobs's inspirational deeds in *Organizing Genius.* Under Jobs, the Mac team became the ultimate heroic underdogs, taking on not only competitors but the nonbelievers inside Apple as well. They were rebels; their spiritual leader, Jobs, raised the pirate flag outside the Macintosh building, and he challenged team Macintosh to put "a dent in the universe." Former Apple CEO John Sculley recalls the same time period in his autobiography *Odyssey:* "Steve's 'pirates' were a handpicked band of the most brilliant mavericks inside and outside Apple. Their mission, as one would broadly describe it, was to blow people's minds and overturn standards. United by the Zen slogan 'The journey is the reward,' the pirates ransacked the company for ideas, parts, and design plans. Steve dreamed up the pirate metaphor, first springing it on his small Mac team in September of 1982. 'It's more fun to be a pirate than to join the Navy,' Steve would say" (Sculley and Byrne, 1988).

The Macintosh group achieved truly remarkable—some, such as Bennis, would even claim impossible—results by combining all the elements cited above. Not only did the members feel *part of a special group,* they were convinced that their *shared mission* was important, not

(continued)

only for themselves but also for all of society. Jobs fanned the inspirational campfires by telling tales of a *common enemy,* using images that evoke epic struggles of light and darkness, much like *Star Wars,* or *The Lord of the Rings.* Casting IBM in the role of the dark foe, Jobs pushed his software development team to superhuman limits. As deadlines approached and programmers worked bleary-eyed around the clock, their leader employed a classic "good and evil" storyline to energize these dedicated team members: "If we don't do it, IBM is going to take over. If having really great products, much better products than theirs, isn't enough to compete with them, then they'll have the whole thing. They'll have the greatest monopoly of all time. . . . If we don't do this, nobody can stop IBM" (Levy, 1995).

Remarkable groups like the Macintosh team go beyond shared meaning to a collective crusade. Harvard management professor Rosabeth Moss Kanter claims that outstanding workgroups or companies often exhibit this cult-like fervor. In her 2002 book, *Evolve!,* one of the most salient points is that the best way to create commitment is to instill a job with meaning, so that employees feel they are making a difference, doing something that truly matters.

References

Bennis, W. G., and P. W. Biederman. *Organizing Genius: The Secrets of Creative Collaboration.* (Reading, MA: Addison-Wesley, 1997).

Kanter, R. M. *Evolve!* (Boston: Harvard Business School Press, 2000).

Levy, S. *Insanely Great: The Life and Time of Macintosh, the Computer That Changed Everything.* (New York: Penguin Books, 1995).

Sculley, J., and J. A. Byrne. *Odyssey: Pepsi to Apple; A Journey of Adventure, Ideas, and the Future.* (New York: Harper & Row, 1988).

ful brand for attracting employees. As you can see, the leadership element is critical to just about everything.

Communicate: Convince Others to Buy In

Working for a transformational leader can be a euphoric experience. He or she makes the team feel as though they are working on a cause that is worthy, noble, important, and something to be proud of. However, none of this happens without exceptional communication skills. John Sadowsky has given this aspect of leadership development a lot of attention. John focuses on the leader as someone with a need to communicate, a deep desire to speak to the heart, rather than just the head of the employee. He explains:

> As a teacher of leadership, and a coach of executives, I have thought a great deal about how transformational leadership happens. While it is true that winning leaders have outstanding communication skills, my view is that modern society has developed a false and exaggerated image of the charismatic leader, the single individual capable of moving others to move mountains. In fact, I have seen few cases of "born" charisma. Instead, the power to inspire others develops over time, a leader becoming charismatic through the force of his message. Not all effective leaders fit the image of the rousing public speaker. Rather, I have found that truly outstanding communication skills have their roots in four characteristics that transformational leaders seem to share:
>
> 1. *Self-knowledge:* Transformational leaders develop clear ideas of who they are, what they believe, and what they stand for. It is only from this firm base of self-knowledge that they can effectively lead others.
>
> 2. *Ongoing self-discovery:* Their sense of self is so clear because they are exceedingly good at processing the lessons of their own life experiences. Learning is a constant, ongoing, and lifelong process.

3. *A longing for self-expression:* More than a desire to lead, they develop the yearning to express themselves, to speak from the heart about matters of deep importance to them. It is through this authentic self-expression that they touch the hearts of their followers.

4. *An ability to lead by autobiography:* Not only do the most effective leaders speak from the heart, their own life stories make them credible and inspirational to others.

In Margaret Thatcher, whose leadership transformed Great Britain in the 1980s, we observe a case of the four characteristics coming together with transformational results. When we read or listen to Thatcher's speeches, we sense someone with a very clear understanding of who she is. From childhood and throughout her life, she processed life's lessons and molded them into a coherent worldview. As a Member of Parliament, and during the campaign to become Prime Minister, her message became powerfully moving and authentic to the electorate. This daughter of a middle-class shopkeeper convinced a nation that her personal values—self-reliance, initiative, and decency—mirrored precisely the principles necessary for putting a "lost" Britain back on course.[2]

Here is another example: Peter Alcide, the business head for Lee Hecht Harrison North America, has had such an experience. In 1996, at Lee Hecht Harrison, Peter first had the occasion to work with Ray Roe. After Ray joined the company, he quickly rose to the position of COO and eventually president. At Lee Hecht Harrison, Ray grew the company's revenue significantly while increasing the profit margin from about 5 percent pretax to upward of 30 percent. When Ray made the necessary changes to bring about this transformation, many long-term employees felt that he was going to destroy the company. Instead, the company became stronger and more productive.

Peter Alcide was the company's CFO at the time. He told me that working with Ray was different because "Ray is a leader, not a manager." Very simply put—that is the difference. Being the CEO does not automatically make one a leader. By basic position description, CEOs "manage." The noted author on leadership Warren Bennis said that management can be taught, but leadership needs to be *learned*. Successfully adopting the transformation leadership approach is valuable in learning to lead.

Let me give you another example: I sold my company to Adecco during Ray Roe's tenure as CEO of Adecco North America. I had been in the recruiting business for 14 years and thought I had a good handle on the industry. During the middle of the Iraq War, I made a comment to Ray that what we were doing in our civilian jobs was hollow. We are both West Point graduates and I told him I felt like I was sitting back here as a civilian while others in the military were doing what the country needed to be done.

Ray is an experienced combat leader—the second person in his West Point class to attain the rank of general; he told me I was wrong. He said, "I don't know about that. I think you're missing the point. What we are doing here is very important. Our companies collectively help thousands—tens of thousands—of people find work every day in this country. On any day in North America alone we have more than a hundred thousand people on our payroll as temporary employees working for our clients—people who benefit greatly from what we do. I think that is tremendously important to the nation and I think you should appreciate what you're doing to make that happen. No, we're not in harm's way in Iraq, but ours is important work just the same."

If I had been in the army, I could have taken any hill he ordered me to. I left his office feeling a little bit taller than when I walked in.

Ray was sold on the vision, believed in what he was doing, and could inspire others to follow his lead. This talent is not alone in our company nor is it exclusive to North America. When Klaus Jacov took the role of chairman and CEO of Adecco Group, South America, the parent company of all the Adecco brands worldwide, he came to the United States and showed us his version of transformational leadership. Klaus Jacov is a huge success. By most accounts, he is a billionaire who could easily be sitting on an estate relaxing away his time. Instead, in his 70s, he stepped in to lead our company. Let me give you an example of how quickly this sort of leadership can begin to change a company for the better. In January 2006, Klaus came to Florida to a meeting of all the regional and area managers of Adecco Group, North America. These are typically young managers early in their careers overseeing a cluster of branch offices. They are the heartbeat of the company. Klaus Jacov stood in front of them in a sports jacket and blue jeans—most of them had never met him until that day. He told them that he had a *dream* and that he wanted them to join in his dream. He spoke of the company's need to attack the competitive marketplace with a newfound vision oriented on a local connection to customers—one on one. Gone was the global sales organization—he had disbanded it. He wanted this group of managers sitting in front of him to be empowered at their level to make a difference for the company.

When he was through with his talk, these young managers could begin to see themselves as leaders. They had truly bought in. This was more than a speech. Because Klaus Jacov *believed*, he was able to appeal to the heart of each of these young leaders. That belief begins the transformational leadership process.

You Have to Be Out Front

You can't lead people who have bought in from behind your desk. This sort of leadership requires you to be out front, showing the others the way. I witnessed this while working with Phil Lynch of the Reuters American group. We handled much of his recruiting. Lynch was inspired by Tom Glocer's vision and was out front putting the Fast Forward process in place. Let me demonstrate how inspired Lynch was. In early 2005, a couple years into the Fast Forward plan, Phil Lynch told me that he was working hard to transform the American organization at Reuters into a client-facing market channel rather than its former, more self-contained operating business unit. He said, "This is what's best for the company." He also went on to say that he was pretty sure that when it was all over he would probably be out of a job as CEO of the American group.

The new business model adopted under Glocer's Fast Forward plan basically left the company's regional leaders in charge of sales channels. They were not going to remain divisional CEOs in the classic sense any longer. But this did not dampen Phil Lynch. He was convinced that this vision was right for the company, and he followed Tom Glocer's lead.

Not every leader is as principled as Phil Lynch. He and I were talking about Dick Grasso's woes at the New York Stock Exchange. I defended Grasso by saying that he had accepted the compensation package he was given by his board—"who would turn that deal down?" Phil said, "Well, I'm not knocking Grasso but I'll tell you I've done it; I turned down a raise just a year ago. Last year I was slotted for a raise but refused it. We were laying people off—how could I take a raise?" Phil Lynch is a young guy with a young family so this was no small decision. This leads me to another aspect of being out front. You must lead with integrity. A quick trip back to West Point puts this very succinctly:

If leaders are not looking for the truth, if situations are not framed as having moral implications in the first place, then these leaders make decisions based on the other criteria, often with disturbing results. Moral sensitivity is not enough. Once leaders recognize that a moral problem exists, then they have to decide what is right. . . .

Without the courage to take action, to DO the right thing . . . all moral awareness and judgment is for naught. . . . True leaders of character . . . "choose the harder right over the easier wrong" over and over again.[3]

There is no room for half-truths, the old wink-and-nod stuff, or the occasional omission just won't work. People will not follow those they can't trust—transformational leaders get people to push the limits of their capabilities. They won't put out the effort for people they don't trust.

An excerpt from the noted leadership scholar Bernard Bass sums this up:

Declaring that ethics is at the heart of leadership, Ciulla (1995) concluded that 'a culture's ethical values are what define the concept of leadership.' Leadership is fundamental to ethical considerations. Again, Gini (1995) avowed that 'without the continuous commitment, enforcement and modeling of leadership, standards of business ethics cannot and will not be achieved in organizations . . . badly led businesses wind up doing unethical things.' Kouzes and Posner (1993) noted that the credibility of leadership depended on its moral purpose, trust, and the hopes it engendered. Leaders are seen as obligated and responsible for the moral environment of their group, organization or society (Greenleaf, 1977). A major task for leaders is bringing together their followers around common values (Fairholm, 1991). The leaders themselves, often are seen as the embodiment of such values (McCollough, 1991). And just as when leaders are more competent, those they lead are more effective, so when leaders are more morally mature, those they lead display higher moral reasoning (Dukerich, Nichols, et al., 1990).[4] (*Note:* References are from the original.)

Strong Ethics Breeds Leaders of Character

In business, the final word has got to be the numbers. All the human capital properly deployed and thoughtfully led is intended to maximize profit and production. When Ray took over Adecco, North America, the company faced some big problems and had not been very profitable. In just 18 months, the numbers emerged to tell the story (Figure 11.2). It is not a story of massive, protracted, time-consuming reengineering. It's Ray's report card as a transformational leader. He needed to take action, take risk, and persuade his team and the Group CEO of Adecco, that his strategy was correct. It is easy in a high-volume business to fall victim to praying at the altar of "top-line revenue growth." These businesses are typically so large in scale that they focus on adding incremental business

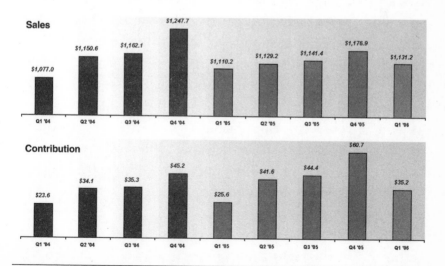

Figure 11.2   Adecco, North America
(In millions USD Constant Currency).

without enough attention on how profitable this new business will be. It is kind of like stoking an engine, just throw on more coal and all will be well. That is not the case, however. Too often the added revenue can actually cost the company money. In these businesses, the margins are razor thin. It takes character to jettison top-line revenue that was not profitable when the top line is a big part of your report card.

Ray realized this very quickly after he assumed his new role. He had to fix some internal controls on the operations side of the business *and* turn the business around at the same time. That was no small feat. What did he do? As the leader, he put the right person in charge of fixing the operational issues—Pete Alcide; and he put the right person in charge of the new approach to sales—Joyce Russell. He went out and talked to customers, and then he went to Europe to let the parent company know what he was doing. What happened? Well, Ray, the South Poler who graduated in the bottom half of his West Point class turned in a very strong report.

The numbers tell the story (Figure 11.2). North American sales were in range over the eight quarters. This company has more than 1,000 offices in North America and thousands of employees. It is not easy to shift something that big. He got rid of most of the unprofitable business that was in the top line and set out to rebook new, more profitable revenue. He also took a reasonable amount of cost out of the business. At the end of the second operating year, profit was up drastically and growing; profit on the same billion or so dollars was up by nearly 33 percent—moving from $45,000,000 to more than $60,000,000 when comparing fourth quarter 2005 with fourth quarter 2006. It was risky to cut the top-line revenue in a world where analysts demand revenue growth every quarter, but it was the right thing to do. I watched it happen. Ray did this by inspiring everyone in the company to do a little better—that goes for his leadership team and the team in the field. When everybody does a little more, *a lot* of good can happen. Transformational leaders will write the next chapter—they'll need to have all the right stuff. The character to make hard choices is a big part of that.

Let's review South Polers. They've suffered, so they have *confidence and character*. They are *communicators*. They are *passionate* and *creative*. They somehow *stand out*. They have all the potential to be great transformational leaders. Go find them or suffer your fate. If *the team fails, the leader fails; and the game is over*.

Downloadable Forms and Tools

All forms and tools are available for download from: www.AlanGuarino.com.

1. The QuickScreen document that follows (Figure 11.3) is highlighted in gray where the user needs to customize it for the specific recruiting assignment at hand.

   When developing the Measuring Questions, use our questions in the example as a guide. By doing so, you will create questions with tight phraseology that block the candidate from giving you subjective (fluff) answers that lack objective, measurable, content.

   Occasionally, after reviewing the QuickScreen, candidates will opt out of the process because they realize they lack the depth that the position calls for either in skills, knowledge, experience, or attributes. This even happens with candidates who feel that they are a perfect fit after hearing your verbal description of the position and reading your write-up of the job.

   Typically, candidates will not try to bluff past the QuickScreen—much of the content you ask for will be valuable during the reference checking phase of the recruiting effort.

2. The quality component of a recruiting project has typically rested solely on the shoulders of the recruiting professional leading the assignment. Our model is highly process driven so that each search is done in accordance with this best practices approach. It ensures a baseline of recruiting quality that the recruiting professional then enhances with their individual expertise. The model (as shown in Figures 11.4 through 11.10) is called the Cornell Candidate Acquisition Model (C-CAM).

QuickScreen™

Position:	Chief Technology Officer
Company Name:	XYZ Corp
Division:	Information Technology
Candidate Name:	Jane Doe
Date:	20th November, 2006

Mission Critical Aspects of the Position:

Our client is one of the world's leading suppliers of business information, services, and research. Its database contains statistics on hundreds of millions of companies in more than two hundred countries. Our client sells that information and integrates it into software products and web-based applications. They also offer marketing information and purchasing-support services.

The CTO role is responsible for leading the technology organization under the CIO to develop new leading-edge applications, plan for the strategic growth, and manage the IT Operations. The successful candidate will foster new ideas by establishing a process for innovation that allows for growth of the business. This will allow for the transformation of the IT organization from "patch and repair" to strategic forward development. Strong leadership, mentoring, and motivation will drive the initiatives for the group.

Figure 11.3 QuickScreen Downloadable Questionnaire Cover Sheet

Measuring Questions:

Given the mission outlined, we seek to measure some key skills, knowledge, and experiences in order to evaluate the candidate's likelihood of success beyond what is found on the resume. We have found that our QuickScreen approach provides an evaluation mechanism that efficiently seeks to measure the match between the candidate and the critical aspects of the position. Questions are posed to candidates as if they are currently employed—we ask candidates who are in transition to approach the questions from their most applicable former employment situation.

We ask that candidates address the following questions for this position:

1. As a member of the executive management team, your counterparts will look to you as a valued colleague helping to set cultural, technological, and operational directions for the organization. Please answer (A) and (B) and discuss specific results.

   (A) Speak to moments in your recent past where you led your organization to deploy technology to enhance business performance.

   (B) Why were the changes needed and what business, cultural, and technological barriers existed?

2. You have previously been involved in the high-level transformation of an IT organization. Give us some examples of how you took the group from "patch and repair" to strategic forward-thinking development.

3. Development of a strong, highly motivated team is critical to moving innovative initiatives forward. Please give examples of direct report employees you have successfully developed. Where are they now?

4. Today, everyone needs to do more with less. How have you implemented best practices and compliance in the technology organization?

5. As a technology leader, how have you partnered with other business unit leadership and what did you do to earn their respect as a business partner?

Cornell Candidate Acquisition Model

C-CAM™

Figure 11.4   C-CAM Slide 1.

C-CAM Process Explained

Phase I – Critical Points: The Search Strategy Process asks the Questions,

- What doe the client want from this position?
- Where will the talent that is needed be found?

An effective search results from a smart plan BEFORE any recruiting calls are made. The QuickScreen, the 80 Targeted Contacts, and the Situation Summary all come from the Search Stragegy Process. Under C-CAM, no recruiting calls should be made in the first 72 hours of the search. During this time period, a target list of 80 contacts should be made. They should include the following:

– Actual Prospective Candidates from Research, Internal Database, and Market Knowledge: 25 names

– Networking Sources:

* 30 peer level individuals from the specialty area you seek (ie. Marketing, CFO, IT, etc.) regardless of industry.

* 15 executive level leaders at a level ABOVE the current position regardless of industry

* 10 people in professional services who provide services to the specialty area you are seeking
(ie. When you are recruiting for a CIO, contact practice leaders at large consulting firms who sell to CIO's. They will know the best talent and have the connections.)

This mix of targets should yield at least 50 actual contacts and 30 additional referrals. The referrals will most likely be top caliber individuals (top 10%\performers) if you have spoken to the right targets. From this set of well planned contacts, you should be able to create a slate that will result in a completed search at least 75% of the time. The other 25% of the time, you will need to re-do this process with about 40 additional contacts to correct the errors in the first effort.

Phase II – In this phase you are actually casting the net for prospects by making the recruiting calls. (other electronic techniques can leverage this including email blasts, news group posting etc). From this effort you begin to evaluate candidates and determine this who should be interviewed. After interviewing, those you feel fit the criteria should complete the QuickScreen. From that, you can then determine your SHORT LIST of candidates recommended to the client for the position.

Phase III– This is where you act as the intermediary between the client and the candidates to manage the communications and ensure the process results in effective exchange of information. During this phase you are promoting the opportunity so that candidates see the career potential and become predisposed to accept an offer if selected.

Phase IV – This is where you orchestrate the completion of the search – determining reasonable compensation arrangements, conducting final references, background checks, etc. and of course preparing the candidate for the counter offer from the current employer so as to avert a successful counter offer.

ALL of these phases require a significant amount of work. The notes above are very superficial explanations of the components of the C-CAM process. Almost every phase requires hours of training for each sub-element of the process and takes years to perfect.

Figure 11.5 C-CAM process explained.

201

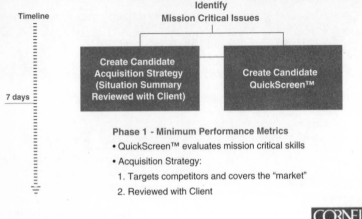

Figure 11.6   Phase 1: Needs assessment.

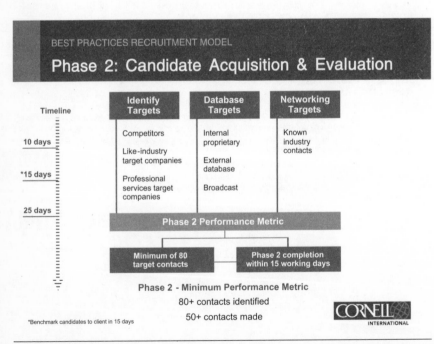

Figure 11.7   Phase 2: Candidate acquisition and evaluation.

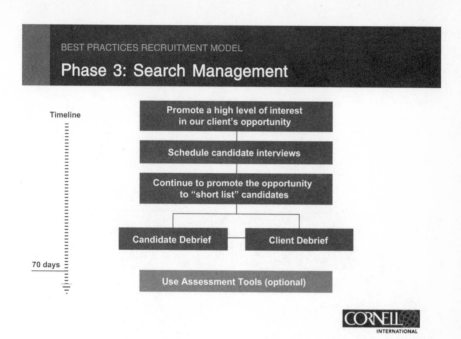

Figure 11.8 Phase 3: Search management.

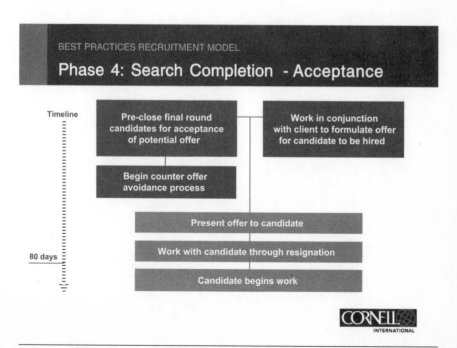

Figure 11.9 Phase 4: Search completion—Acceptance.

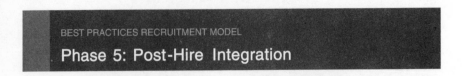

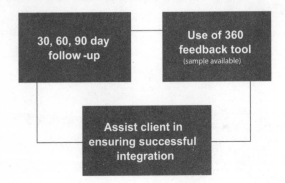

Figure 11.10   Post-hire integration.

EPILOGUE

A cademics is not a team sport. Ponder that for a second. The future of successful business requires that bright, creative people work effectively as a team. The current paradigm in most areas of formal education is one of Darwinian, competitive self-promotion sometimes even at the expense of others. There are businesses where these traits can be effective, but not too many. Most business situations call for the ability to team with others.

The academic community—that is, mainstream educational institutions of higher education and public schools—is failing our society. The public schools are held ransom by teachers' unions that appear to perpetuate mediocrity (albeit with the best intentions)—why else would a union resist efforts to provide "merit" pay for outstanding performance? That would mean that teachers could actually be judged as average, above average, or below average. That would mean that rather than tenure, a teacher would need to perform to maintain his or her teaching job. I don't just fault the unions. I fault the administrators. Think about that word for a minute—*administrators*. Some of them are in charge of $200 million operations. Can you imagine any CEO referring to herself or himself as an administrator? I don't think so!

No, we need educators who are accountable for the work they do in the classrooms and for the results they get. We need administrators who are leaders helping educators put out an amazing product, who find ways to create a first-class learning environment in the school facilities, who set high standards for students and teachers and create positive environments of challenge and reward. We need administrators who inspire teachers just as CEOs are expected to inspire their employees in corporations.

When it comes to higher education, we need colleges that are more interested in the future potential of the applicant than they are in the impact that the applicant's SAT scores will have on their college's rankings. I am sure with all the intellect in higher education, someone can figure out a way to assess a student's potential for high achievement. The fact that many colleges refuse to have applicant interviews is a clear example that the colleges are interested in the scores, the paper, and not the person. I wonder if those admissions officers would respect a college who hired them solely from the data on their resumes without ever having met them.

Our academic system drives the early development of our most valuable business resource, and it is failing us. It blocks out students with high potential but low scores. It dishes out theories from people who have never done what they are teaching others to do. It is held back by a century-old inertia that needs to be broken. We need academic leaders and educators who create curriculums that foster teamwork. Dropping athletic programs that teach teamwork, schools are doing little in the curriculum to create future employees who can work together effectively and understand each other's strengths and weaknesses.

The business world spends hundreds of millions, perhaps billions of dollars remediating what should have been taught in school. This is both a social and an economic issue that needs attention *now.*

NOTES

Chapter 1   The Global Talent Market: Why Our Nation's Graduates Will Work for Wipro in India and Why It Matters to Everyone

1. Thomas Friedman, The World Is Flat (New York: Farrar, Straus, and Giroux, 2005).
2. *Fortune* (February 6, 2006), 48.

Chapter 2   The Past Is Gone, the Future Is Now, and the Talent Age Is upon Us

1. Peter Capelli, *The New Deal at Work* (Boston, MA: Harvard University Press, 1999).
2. Erica J. Bever, Elizabeth Stephenson, and David W. Tanner, "How India's Executives See the World," *McKinsey Quarterly* (Special Edition, 2005).

Chapter 3   Hire from the South Pole

1. Paul Orfalea, *Copy This* (New York: Workman, 2005), 137.
2. See note 1, 136.

Chapter 4   Emotional Intelligence Is More Important Than Grade Point Average

1. en.wikipedia.org/wiki/Emotional_intelligence.
2. http://www.ihhp.com/business_case.htm.

3. Cary Chemiss, paper presented at the Annual Meeting of the Society for Industrial and Organizational Psychology, New Orleans, LA, April 15, 2000.

4. Goleman, Daniel, *Working with Emotional Intelligence* (New York: Bantam, 1998).

5. Dale Carnegie, *How to Win Friends and Influence People* (New York: Simon & Schuster, 1936).

Chapter 5   Five South Pole Talent Secrets

1. Paul Orfalea, *Copy This* (New York: Workman, 2005), xiii.

2. See note 1, xxi.

3. Erica J. Bever, Elizabeth Stephenson, and David W. Tanner, "How India's Executives See the World," *McKinsey Quarterly* (Special Edition, 2005).

4. http://urel.binghamton.edu/PressReleases/2003/may-jun03/Commencement.html (May 1, 2003).

Chapter 6   The Human Resources Division: Finally, a Chance to Shine

1. Deloitte & Touche USA LLP, "Winning the New Talent Game: Talent Management Strategies," January 18, 2006.

2. E-mail from Michael Foster, Human Capital Institute.

Chapter 7   Strategize to Optimize Talent: Talent Road Mapping and the Talent Inventory

1. From an interview with Peter Louch, 2005.

2. See note 1.

Chapter 8   Attract South Polers and Other Talent: Find the Needle in the Haystack

1. Christine Johnson, Director of Employee Communications, "Stand for Something—Stand Out with Your Employer Brand," http://www.shaker.com/in/sfs.html.

2. From an interview with Cormac Culihane, March 2006.

3. www.brainbench.com/xml/bb/business/hiring/products overview/xml.

Chapter 10   Deploy Cutting-Edge Methods for Staff Development: Invest in Human Capital

1. From an interview with Louis Csoka, June 2006.

2. Robert Rigby-Hall, the global head of HR at Lexis Nexis.

3. Data-Driven Dialogues is a registered trademark of eePulse, Inc., part of Data and Dialogue Driven Leadership™.

4. T. M. Welbourne, "Learning about Leadership and Firm Growth through Monthly Data Collection and Dialogue with Entrepreneurs," *International Entrepreneurship and Management Journal,* Vol. 2, No. 1 (2006).

5. T. M. Welbourne, "Data and Dialogue Driven (3D) Leadership: The Future Path for HR Pioneers," *World at Work Journal* (February 2004), 55–61.

Chapter 11   Lead: Follow Me and Do as I Do

1. John Sadowsky and Loïck Roche, "Leadership Best Practice: Providing a Sense of Deeper Purpose," *Business Leadership Review,* Vol. 2, No. 3 (2005).

2. For a more detailed discussion of Thatcher's transformational leadership, see: H. Gardner and E. Laskin, *Leading Minds: An Anatomy of Leadership* (New York: BasicBooks, 1995).

3. "Cadet Leadership Development System," USMA Circular 1, June 10, 2002, p. 29.

4. Bernard Bass, "The Ethics of Transformational Leadership," *KLSP: Transformational Leadership,* working papers (College Park, MD: Academy of Leadership Press, 1997).

Invitation to Contact Me

I am happy to discuss any recruiting or human resources related topics that cross your mind. Feel free to call or e-mail me and I'll do my best to get back to you within 24 hours.

I can be reached at (845) 236-3986 or e-mail: Alan@AlanGuarino.com.

I look forward to hearing from you!

Index

A

Academic system, flaws in, 205–206
Adecco North America, 189, 193–194
Agere Systems, 104
Agility, developing, 173–175
Alcide, Peter, 188–189, 194
Alger, Horatio, xiii–xiv
America Online, 44
Apex Performance, 165–170
Apple Computer, 185
Auto industry, Japan and, 10

B

Baby Boomers, replacing, 90–91
Banker's Trust Company, 164
Bank of New York, The, 41, 44, 85–86, 164
Bass, Bernard, 192–193
Bear Stearns, 73, 127
Bennis, W. G. (*Organizing Genius*), 185
Bever, Erica, 22, 74

Biederman, P. W. (*Organizing Genius*), 185
Blockbuster Video, 46
Blumberg, Anthony, 34
Bradley, Omar, 154
Bradt, George (*Hot Landings: Challenging New Leadership Roles*), 157, 170–172
Brainbench Employment Testing, 145
Branding, 115–146
  components of, 120
  methodology, 120–121
Branson, Richard, 46
Brockovich, Erin, 46
Brown, Anthony (Tony), 72–73
Business savvy, 31–32
Byrne, J. A. (*Odyssey*), 185

C

Cappelli, Pete (*The New Deal at Work*), 11–12, 19–20
Carnegie, Dale (*How to Win Friends and Influence People*), 58–59
Cattani, Andrea, 35–36

China, college graduates in, 11
China, threat from, 19
Commander's intent, 182
Communication, importance
　　of, 59–60, 64–65
Copy This (Paul Orfalea), 30,
　　66–68
Corcoran, Barbara, 45, 55, 72,
　　75–77
Cornell Candidate Acquisition
　　Model, 136–137
Csoka, Louis, 166–170
Culihane, Cormac, 123, 125–126

D

Dell, Michael, 41, 54
Dell Computers, 54
Deloitte Touche, 16–17
Deutsche Bank, 164
Dumas, Paul, 104

E

Eisenhower, Dwight, 154
Eisner, Michael, 55
Emotional Intelligence (Daniel
　　Goleman), 52, 58
Emotional intelligence (EI):
　　definition of, 51
　　productivity and, 52
　　theory of, 30–32, 56–60
Employer brand, creating a,
　　115–146
Engels, Max, 3

Entry level jobs, recruiting for,
　　126–127
Ethics, 193–195
European Union, threat from,
　　18–19
Evolution, 8
Evolve! (Rosabeth Moss Kanter),
　　186
ExxonMobil, 15

F

Fast Feedback Leadership,
　　175–176
Fast Forward process, 191
Fidata, Inc., 41
Financial capital, importance
　　of, 15–16
Ford, 15
Ford, Henry, 53–54
Foster, Michael, 95
Frick, Henry Clay, 53
Friedman, Thomas (*The World
　　Is Flat*), 8–9, 31

G

Gagan, Kevin, 173–173
Gardner, Howard, 56
General Electric, 41–42
Gioia, Jamie, 41–42
Global economy, America's
　　chances in, 9–10
Globalization, talent and, 6–7,
　　21–22

Glocer, Tom, 183–185, 191
Goat, West Point's, 42–44
Go Daddy, 46
Goldman Sachs, 35
Goleman, Daniel (*Emotional Intelligence, Working with Emotional Intelligence*), 30, 52, 57–58
Gonzalez, Dan, 92–93
Grant, Hiram (Ulysses S.), 38–39
Grasso, Dick, 191
Greenberg, Alan C. (*Memos from the Chairman*), 128

H

Hamilton, Alexander, 86
Harrington, Richard, 106, 108
Harrison, Steve, 181
Hay Group, The, 145
Helmsley, Leona, 56
Hertzberg theories, 92
Hoffman, Bob, 33, 35–36
Hot Landing approach, 170–172
Hot Landings: Challenging New Leadership Roles (George Bradt), 157, 170
How to Win Friends and Influence People (Dale Carnegie), 58–59
Hubbard, Elbert, 27
Huizenga, Wayne, 46
Human Capital Institute (HCI), 19, 94–85, 149, 155

Human resources department:
development of, 83–87
predicting talent, 87–90
structure of, 89
Human resources model, 95–96

I

India:
college graduates in, 11
threat from, 19
Wipro and, 11
Institute for Health and Human Potential, 52
Interviewing, art of, 130–135

J

Jackson, Stonewall, 37
Jacov, Klaus, 190
Japan, auto industry and, 10
Jennings, Peter, 46
JetBlue, 46
Jobs, Steve, 55, 60, 185–186
Johnson, Christine, 117–118
Johnson, John H., 65
Johnson, Tom, 10
Johnson Publishing Company, 65

K

Kamen, Dean, 74–75
Kanter, Rosabeth Moss (*Evolve!*), 186

Kinko's, 30
Kinsey, Jim, 44
Kizilos, Mark, 106–107
Korn Ferry, 123–124
Koshiba, Masatoshi, 46

L

Lasker, Bunny, 128
Lasn, Kalle, 186–186
Leader, how to be, 58–59
Leadership, 181–196
Leadership, commander's
    intent, 182
Leadership, positive, 182
Lee, Robert E., 37–39
Lee Hecht Harrison, 87–88,
    145, 172–173, 175–176,
    188
Lehman Brothers, 73
Levy, Gus, 128
Lewis, Cy, 128
Lexis Nexis, 172
Lincoln, Abraham, 37–40
Louch, Peter, 103–105
Lynch, Phil, 191

M

Madison, James, 7
Management, talent and, 92–94
Marx, Karl, 3, 6, 7, 8
Mayer, John, 57
McCarthy, Kathleen, 106–107
McNabb, Donavan, 155–156

Memos from the Chairman (Alan
    C. Greenberg), 128
Merrill Lynch, 34
Montgomery, Bernard, 153
Morgan Stanley, 34
Mosaic Capital, 184
*My Battle for Survival from Mlyny
    to Melbourne* (Godel
    [Wroblewski] Wroby), 68

N

Neeleman, David, 46
Neuman, William, 77
New Deal at Work (Pete
    Cappelli), 11–12, 19–20
Newton, Isaac, 57

O

Odyssey (John Sculley), 185
Orbeta, J. P., 119
Orfalea, Paul (*Copy This*), 30,
    66–68, 127
Organizing Genius (W. G. Bennis
    and P. W. Biederman), 185
Orwell, George (*1984*), 54
Owens, Terrell, 155–157

P

Parsons, Bob, 46
Parsons Technology, 46
Patton, George, 68–69, 149–154

Peak Performance Center,
    167–170
Pennington, Kevin, 106
Performance Enhancement
    Center, West Point's, 167
Perna, Tom, 41
Pershing, Blackjack, 153–154
Personnel department. *See*
    Human resources division
Power down, 182
PrimeGenesis, 170
Product direction, 124–125
Productivity:
    change in, 5–6
    emotional intelligence and,
        52

Q

QuickScreen approach,
    129–130, 135, 138–145,
    197–205

R

Recruiting:
    campus, 126–127
    talent inventory and,
        103–105
Recruitment solutions, 121–123,
    125
Reuters, 183–185
Reverse behavioral assessment,
    159
Rigby-Hall, Robert, 172

Roche, Loick, 184
Rockefeller, John D., 45
Roe, Ray, 188–190, 193–194
Rogers Communication, 106
Rommel, Erwin, 153–154
Russell, Joyce, 194

S

Sadowsky, John, 184, 187
Salovey, Peter, 57
Sculley, John (*Odyssey*), 185
Shaffer, Dave, 70–71
Shaker Corporation,
    117–118
Smith, Adam, 40, 86
Soleil Securities, 35
South Pole, case study,
    36–40
South Polers, description of,
    63–67
South Pole theory, 63–77
Standard Oil Company, 45
Stellato, Bob, 33, 35
Stephenson, Elizabeth, 22, 74
Sternberg, Robert J., 30
Street smarts, definition of, 31
Success, equation for, 32

T

Talent:
    as an asset, 29
    investing in, 163–177
    marketing, 115–146

Talent *(Continued)*
  predicting, 87–90
  secrets of, 63–77
  under attack, 17–20
Talent Age, beginnings of,
    23–24
Talent Inventory, 101–102
Talent market, supply and
    demand and, 21
Talent Road Mapping,
    101–111
Tanner, David W., 22, 74
Thatcher, Margaret, 49, 188
Thomson Corporation, 70–71,
    160–111
Time Warner, 123–124
Tipping points, 173–174
Tolstoy, Leo (*War and Peace*),
    45
Transformational leadership,
    190–192
Twain, Mark, 179

U

U.S.Bancorp, 42

V

Velli, Joe, 44
Vemo, 103–105
Virgin Corporation, 46

W

War and Peace (Leo Tolstoy),
    45
Watson Wyatt, 118–199
Wechsler, David, 56, 60
Welch, Jack, 56
West Point, Goat in the class,
    42–44
Winner, defining, 32–33
Wipro, 11
Workforce planning, 105–106
*Working with Emotional
    Intelligence* (Daniel
    Goleman), 52
World Is Flat, The (Thomas
    Friedman), 8–9
Wroby (Wroblewski), Godel
    (*My Battle for Survival from
    Mlyny to Melbourne*), 68